ABSOLUTELY
POETRY
ANTHOLOGY
2

Edited by

Steve Wheeler
Imelda Zapata Garcia
John Rennie

First published by
Wheelsong Books
4 Willow Close,
Plymouth PL3 6EY,
United Kingdom

Book design © Steve Wheeler, 2022
Cover artwork © Katie Collins, 2022

First published in 2022

Print ISBN: 979-8-40797-979-1

Foreword

Welcome to our second anthology. Thank you for taking the time to read these heartfelt pieces of art. The Absolutely Poetry group takes pride in offering a platform — a space — to poets who otherwise might feel uncomfortable or unsafe in posting such deeply personal writing. We have a zero tolerance for bullying and take great care in protecting our members. We are a group of international poets who hail from across five different continents, a diverse group of artists dedicated to an art which we consider monumental in today's society. The poems in this volume were written by members ranging from 11 to 94 years of age.

When we announced this second anthology, we were inundated with more than 430 submissions. This is a positive thing in that we can now make preparations for a third anthology. The objective of the anthology is a great humanitarian one. All proceeds from direct sales of this book will go to an international charity fund. Save The Children has already profited from the sales of our first anthology, when they funded a camel library for unschooled children in Ethiopia.

Thanks to readers like you, we are inspired to continue producing such books. We truly appreciate your continued support with this venture.

Imelda Zapata Garcia
Poet and Co-Founder
Absolutely Poetry Facebook Group

The Soul of Beginning
Rafik Romdhani

Governments feed on the dreams
of the unborn generations
And pitch like crows their tents
which they call parliaments.
What will the distant dream eat?
How will the unborn colour the bull skin
tread by demons with legs of fire and sin
while drowning in the deepest ashes
of sincerity after Didon's self-burning?
Governments dig their people's graves
with the teeth of mellifluous promises.
Every speech is under the shining
of a crying camera, over choked chimeras
in putting up with bitter drowning
in the fickle face of political chiromancy.
The future is fodder for governments' hunger
and a crunched picture holding danger.
After each photo under lights is taken
and each word spoken, mockeries awaken
like a desperate end in the soul of beginning.

Joy
Martin Pickard

Brightly painted eggs hide in the flowerbeds
Distant chiming bells bring soft whipped 99's
Paper castle flags add grandeur to the shore
Spooky clothes and masks fill bags
with sweets and treats
Newly minted conkers shine brightly in your hand
Fiery metal wands trace figures in the park
Crackling paper treasure troves rustle in the stocking
Milestones of childhood joyfulness
that mark the path of time

The Brooklyn Theater, 1876
Rob Krabbe

It was always so very crowded there.
The "joint hoppin'" and hot like fire.
Ghosts of legends travel the cold halls.
Artful; ethereal and masterful through time,
eternally blessing and cursing the sublime.

The spirits in this place, seek their way home.
For each, the show ended; the curtain torn.
Of players working the stage; stars were born.
The memories of patrons, had a life of their own;
the sounds still echo, like the ghosts in the storm.

Just as the wind blows through the trees,
the applause frantic like the autumn leaves,
the crowd always screamed for more.
The fire breaks out every single night,
audience and players, hundreds galore!
The excitement itself almost burst right through,
the roof, the walls and bust open the door.

They lived hard; a time of muscle and brawn.
They played hard in this great haunted hall.
The debauchery burned bright from dusk till dawn.
Never a closing show, or a single curtain call.
The dark spirit of The Brooklyn lives on, and on.

So long ago now, no-one much remembers.
Audience, musicians, players and members.
300 souls were lost, and not much was found.
The night The Brooklyn burned to the ground.
Nothing was left, death-cold every ember;
1876, the fifth night of December.

Time Flies
Pureheart Wolf

Tick tock, tick tock,
The hours go by,
Tick tock, tick tock,
I stare at a dead fly.
Tick tock, tick tock,
A waste of a day.
The clock watches,
Tick tock, tick tock,
Weary and weak,
Just like the dead fly,
The watcher of the clock.
Tick tock, tick tock.
Life and death all in time,
Tick tock, tick tock,
No-one pays heed to the moment,
Time flies.

With Just One Page
Vincent Blaison

Slivers of a tree
Painted with words
Of people's hearts
Coming together
To lift a struggling child up

Though storms bring heavy rainfall
The sun will surely break through the mist
And shower joy to the world
Bringing warmth and loving togetherness

With each moment, brings new opportunities
To become a path to newfound gratitude of Grace
If only we could be so blessed
To be able to, just for your sake

Esperanza
Kwaku Adjei-Fobi

I took in all the light
each shaft of it, Ra rays
celebrating birth of day, reflecting faith
I caught the hint in the eye,
raw suckle, straw strength, green sprout...
left speechless, sprawling in the void
Life's screening room, Histories unfurl...
watch whispers, listen to sight's tale
stomp and gate-crash history
the Mona Santa touches me at places
and Esperanza ballets in 3D,
I watch, little-fancied, waiting on Hope
the chain arrives at the hugging sprocket,
ilk and like, matter and splinter,
and Time arrives, full circle at portal of the Soul
Seeking Hallelujahs in the most unthinkable place?
Come sing with me! You and you. Us.
We can trace Ra's rays
out of this dark phase.

Dangerous Pride
Marlo D. Mahair

Some people have been brought up groomed and taught,
Freedom of speech is something easily purchased or bought,
Unbeknownst in her self-petted ego and perilous lies,
She rains on the sun and all that might shine,
To beautify her insecure and angry disposition,
She makes life worse with her tired nasty opposition,
So if you feel uncomfortable with anything I just said,
Maybe you should look to the words boldly written in red,
If Jesus heard you speak he surely would cry,
You are only showing the world a reflection
of your dangerous pride.

Contemplate
Martin Eoghan

Breathe deeply so,
do it ever so slow,
watch shutes of barley
slowly as they grow,
over hills and mountains,
and under the hedgerows,
breathe deeply so,
do it ever so slow.
Those emerald forests
evergreen enchanted leaves,
stay alive and vibrant,
even in the winter's freeze.
Lilacs blooming by the window,
lilies cradled together for show,
breathe deeply so,
do it ever so slow.
Watching water run,
through sediment rock,
time to take in stock,
gather the things you know,
breathe deeply so
do it ever so slow.

Karma
Lisa Combs Otto

He attempted to forgive her sins,
But they weren't his
to name or to release.
Her sins were her own beast to slay.
She didn't mind them.
So in her next life
...she'll pay.

Autumn Dreams
Lynne Truslove

The faintest breath caresses my cheek, my hair slightly tousled, skin tingling from your touch. Knowing there's just you and me, locked into this one perfect moment of time. The universe slumbers while we dance gracefully, in tune with each other's souls. You sigh gently against my neck, a chill travels through my body. I smile and see you, enveloping me entirely. I wish time could stand still, just for a moment, as I dream of the future. But alas it doesn't, you change direction and cause a stir in my heart. My eyes close as I fall into your path. Oh autumn how I love thee, the colours, the fragrant aromas you bring. What could be more perfect I hear you whisper through the trees. My reply is simple, quietly spoken, barely more than a sound, to spend each day in your company, sharing my dreams with my best friend, my rock, my true one love. With that, you whip my hair against my face, leaving me with a gentle kiss. Goodbye for now, but I will return soon, to read the next chapter of the story.

Bamboo
Sofie Linn

He's overprotective and sweet,
big and strong;
gives you all the love he can share
a beautiful soul,
a beautiful spirit.
I hug him and whisper to him
"Please never leave me!"
I see him lying down
drool dripping from his mouth
Struggling to breathe.
A night of tears and sadness.
But you never really left
You'll always be by my side
till the end of time.

The Invisible Child
Imelda Zapata Garcia

Gripping tightly to my night sheets, shaking even while
in slumber, I lay, ever by her side.
Be it now or bygone ages, past all youth, until tomorrow,
every pillow must be shared each endless night.
There's no breath, I feel, no movement, no warm touch
is left, no frame, just a sense of lingering sorrow.
Though I see no ghostly sessions, never fear her lasting
presence, just embrace she'll come again tomorrow.
I grow aged, tired and worn, throughout the pace of clocks
Clocks that tick tock, tick, tick then slowly tock.
Thin skinned, folds, wrinkles pilling up my neck,
down the spine of tired bones, that crick, crack, crock.
She lays fresh, pristine, lily white, her gown on alabaster skin.
Two or three, not quite four, no more.
Ageless wonder, pleasant smile upon pale lips.
Lips which move ever so slightly, gently, slowly,
barely parting, long enough to break a sweet girl's
smile. Touching deep, penetrating scars, healing
wounds left long ago. Fading with every single
time spent there beneath my sheets, between
my love and me. When silence falls, like velvet
curtains, heavy over lids that hide no vision of
a dimming glow, a quieting glimmer languidly
leaving, yet appearing simply to linger to the end.

Who Won Again?
Kevin Walton

Fledged, in flight.
Thriving, yet still angling.
Trajectories and vectors consume focus,
near entirely.
Flat reflective surface
reflects and reveals at once;
revelation like the cast of dice,
flaunting chance like the addict's fix.

Oblivious to odds, winged and majestic,
ravenous in single minded swoop,
angler clutches now quarry,
gullet only, awaiting its thrashings.
How came such intersection?
Fortuitous, on the one talon,
not so much for the impaled,
less so still for the consumed, it "seems."
Random crossings occur,
even as words
reach a reader's eyes;
they breach like bubbles in a boil.
"Unbeknownst" is their
character and calling card both;
only prophets and liars
speak the future in the now.
The pierced, the fed and full,
both, contribute to each's flow
and are bound
in a moment's enclosure.
Valuation of who feeds,
and who eats,
derives a number
equal to itself.
The arithmetic is stark.
One finite life,
divided by so many risks,
and finally subtracted.
That thing on the wing,
life coursing in its veins,
flies on to more peril,
and, its right but avoided end.
That thing consumed,
exuding nothing, lifeless and swallowed,
Is freed,
Into a beginning.
Hunter, hunted,
The angled for and the extracted,
all keep accurate account;
No one won.

You Minus Me Equals Blue
J Davies

Take away the sky and
Clouds could never roam
Take away the trees
And birds would have no home
Everything has a reason,
An equation that is true
And you minus me equals blue.
The hour needs a minute,
The willow needs to cry
A question needs an answer
And that's the reason why
We need to be together —
One becoming two
And you minus me equals blue.
Winter works with red and white
Like berries in the snow
Summer is an artist's dream,
Her colours all on show
And autumn would be bleak and cold
Without her leaves to view
And you minus me equals blue.

Tear Drops
Jon Ware

my bloody teardrops
fall for all the failing crops
and peoples crying
mankind's morality rots
putrefying and dying

23

Wreckage of the Sky

Steve Wheeler

Sadness broods above me,
the bright dawn obfuscated
by a bland roiling of cloud, suspended
like old hoisted sails; grey white
unwashed detritus of the sky;
Filthy cotton wads displayed
on high to grieve and rankle;
discarded in haste to taint
the blue with its haphazard wreckage.
Such grey will not easily disperse;
it loiters with intent above, like
a chronic respiratory disease, or
a mysterious indelible stain.
Bland and colourless in its abandon,
the shards and soiled remnants
of a celestial garage sale,
ripped and ruined beyond redemption
in the least wanted section;
Oh, such insipid oppression;
what spiteful inertia;
to foil the beauty of the
sun's benevolent smile, and
deny the promise of its warmth.
What ingrate vapour of ill repute!
How unwelcome it is, this damp
blanket of gunmetal grey,
this wreckage of the sky.

Love Bleeds

Jon Ware

what does it all mean?
love so bittersweet at times
emotions through rhymes
hearts throbbing just to be seen
bleeding ink as the clock chimes

Universal Resonance
James C. Little

When one beholds
the first pale speck of day
fast blanching out
a fading morning star
which must the brooding night repay,
the tingles of a universe afar
excite the same
in beings of this earth;
a resonance simpatico exact
to echo memories about Thy worth,
recalling—not just deja vu but fact;
reminding—souls
of perfect right unmarred.
It holds the Son of God in high regard;
vibrates its pulse right down to me,
here in my yard.

Crystalline Tears
Cosmic Birch

Crystalline tears
Settle like icicles
on ruddy cheeks
As winter climbs bony limbs
The mountains sigh
in shades of white
And the coldest shadows ruminate
Grasping far off thoughts
Freezing each one
As a drop of dew
Quietly bejewelling the grass
With iridescent dreams
In readiness for a season
Of renewed warmth and release

Pity!

Stuart Dann

Sitting on a bench one day.
This poor old lady passed my way.
Dirty hair, her clothes a tatter.
I softly asked her: What's the matter?
I have lived my life so leave me be.
Was what she then replied to me.

Please my dear come take a seat.
Relieve the strain, just rest your feet.
For I have seen your years of strife.
Having watched you all your life.
In years gone by as you did grow.
The kindest heart that you did show.

Your life is ending, you're now with me.
Take my hand, you shall be free.
Gazing at her puzzled face.
I said now heaven is your place.
I am the Lord down from above.
That's filled with angels full of love.

This upward stairway you now see.
Come take your last walk please with me.
You belong there by my side.
Amongst the other good who've died.
I am too weak to climb that high.
Lord, do I really need to die?

You need not fear my words are true.
For when you tire I'll carry you.
Then my Lord Please set me free.
I'm glad that you have come for me.
It's time for us to leave together.
So you can be in peace forever.

Night Visions

John Rennie

...yet I'd clearly love to say
She danced before my eyes
Peripherally anyway
For no matter how I tried
As I turned to gaze upon
Her distant and yet still
Quiet vision, she'd gone
Leaving nothing but ill
Will and a forlorn desire
To chase beyond reality
But I'm now oh so tired
Caught between duality
Why would she not await
The smallest time of linger
She smiles mockery again
As her elusive fingers
Reach out to mine, denying
So gentle a meaningful
Touch of souls combined
As our gravitations could,
Would, as fated, pull
Us inexorably apart
I turned to see, fateful,
The brightest of stars
And again she was gone
I gazed to every blind side
She was ne'er seen by none
Was it merely by
The tears in my eyes?
I tried, oh how I tried
But with each spin she turned
Her back on our dark side
By her bleakness was I spurned
But I'll forever gaze above
To heavens so distant
Silence, unrequited love
And a sideways glance given
In the deepest of dark nights
I imagine I can still see her

Yet the day's light still fights
And inevitably will conquer.

Shall We Dance?
Kim Elizabeth Dawson

Shall we dance this life of ours?
Shall we tango through the years?
We'll rumba through the happy times
And cha-cha through the tears.
We'll salsa through the sleepless nights
And waltz through teenage doom
And when we have our empty nest
We'll jive in every room!
And when the reaper comes to call
We'll foxtrot in his face
We'll shine our shoes and give a wave
And tap dance happily to our grave.

Sweet Slumber
Tammy Hendrix

I woke to the twining of fingers
snaking beneath warm blankets
following the arching of my leg
risen slightly
gliding curves
dividing valleys
in search of rivers.
Warm breezes burrow
kissing through locks of autumn
whispering, "I love you"
as we lay
bodies pressed and curled
twined and penetrating
drifting off together
I think, how much I love
when you come home late.

Cursed Moon

Anthony Arnold

It's happening again. No! No!
My blood boils
My heart is racing
My flesh torn asunder

It who lives inside begs to come out
I can no longer fight it
I feel it take control of me
I am no longer myself

I feel as if I am in a fog
Here but not here
I scc yct I am blind
I hear yet I am deaf

All because of this cursed moon
Full, a silvery orb in the night sky
A bane of my existence
The jailer of my soul

Unspeakable things I do this night
Yet I don't know, nor do I care
I am not in control
There is no control

Sunlight. Blessed sunlight
The change again comes
I am again human
Human? I will never be human

I again walk the streets
Trying to live
Until again I feel the call
Of the cursed moon

Burnt Like Ashes
Brian Keith

I was burnt like ashes
Pulled like demons
I was thoughtful like sorrow
Attacked in my dreams

I am a nightmare of life
A scream when jolted awake
I am afraid of everything
The hands that shiver and shake

I can be a friend like no other
A companion to souls
I can run into your arms
My emotions can take control

Don't let your life slip away
When tied up by misfortune
Don't push friends away
Gather in every love in proportion

Single Flower Spray
Brett Walker

This wilted flower no longer blooms
A decaying stem in a heart-shaped room
Where once blossomed love, a desolate tomb
Color-faded petals float into greying gloom
My love already dying, my soul follows soon
This desecrated soil, too barren to reap
Like memories long gone, these roots run deep
Salted tears of life's grief, I continue to weep
Into the cracked foundation they silently seep
The once fragrant aroma I promise to keep
Toss this remnant of life upon wooden lid
Limp the flower lays, finally outlived
Next, sprinkle briny dirt, sour n' acrid
To bury all feelings that I've always hid
For it is, farewell and adieu, to you, that I bid

———

Venomous
Sheri Lemay

Angry words fly
Like tiny daggers
Venomous bile spewed
Derogatory, meant to break
Like the lashes of a whip
Leaving marks unseen
Each more painful than the last
Your target becomes numb
Silently weeping
Tears unseen
Not a whimper you hear
Apologies made
Self-hatred expressed
False remorse
Too little
Too late
You won the game
Your opponent unaware
A game was being played

A Storm is Coming
Anthony Arnold

A Storm is coming
People are tired
People will no longer
Accept the status quo
A Storm is coming
The winds of change are blowing
No longer
Can we just
Let it go
Killed in the streets
In our homes
Because of so-called mistakes
Because they just don't care
A Storm is coming

I Fell in Love

Pureheart Wolf

I was taken out for lunch today,
smiled, all the day long,
ordered my favourite from the menu
While listening to my favourite song.
Took a walk along the shore,
Staring at the sea,
The moonlight glistened in the water,
As if smiling back at me.
The feel of sand between my toes,
I felt a love so sweet.
Gentle words, so softly spoken.
My lover, I did meet.
I didn't realise I was special,
I didn't admit defeat.
Time has healed a trauma
With a wound that was cut deep.
I fell in love with me today,
I took myself for lunch.
I spent my time on healing.
A rendezvous, romance.

Dew

James C. Little

Sound and fury is an evanescent flame
fanned high and dry by desiccating wind.
Our mortal vapors soar aloft,
are glad to Heaven's steps ascend
and with the rising sun reclaim
eternal dividend.
The sky is steam from others left before:
Its beads coat all; earth's dew restore.
To face day's lamp and walk with Thee
is evermore a guarantee
of pleasant strolls among the nebulae;
for then, death's shadows fall-backside of me!

Step Child
Octobias Obie Mashigo

O, step child
I feel your aches
Pain that it is haunting your
happiness night and day,
Pain that hate seeing you date
a sunny conversation with friends

When it sees blissful smiles
Swim on your poor face,
It drown them with hateful words
That are hurting you to the core of
Your heart,

It enjoys seeing you in tears
Of yesterday's sorrows
Rolling you into dust of anger,
Stripping you your dignity
Wiping off your identity

O, step child
Chill out
You are not out on this journey
Of life,
Be strong don't let tears
Stroll with joy on your face
To satisfy aches
They bringing to your life,
Pain that is paying a visit to
Ruin a beautiful make up
        smile
 that hide your sadness on
 your face

Cause
You were born for a purpose
Not for people to oppose your
Purpose in this life

Desert

Vee Maistry

The lone and thirsty desert craves
Dew drops of shimmering heavenly bliss
But instead the merciless orb that burns
Every grain a wailing pain
Rolling dunes and endless grains
The 'Ship of the Desert' that challenge and mock
With man at its helm a mocking shame
Dreary and bare it silently beckons
For little minions to stamp and play
On sun-baked grains that tears forsake
The trees and blooms that hide in gloom
And the sterile clouds that cannot birth
As it aches for stubble grass and chunky trees
Alas! The desert an arid land
That wallow in sadness forever doomed

My Ark

James C. Little

I keep my heart inside a box
which floats in the water of His Life.
It makes for us a Holy Ark
that shines as waxed with Spirit's spark,
protects both me and too my heart
from sin's insults,
so we won't be an easy mark
for evil work of the occults.
God sent a star to watch my chest,
and made a covenant with me:
that trust in Him would make us blest
and happy in the Temple be,
to love our Christ, His Cross, and Piety;
to glory in Great Heaven's Best,
you see.

Romantic Shadows

Naomi Tangonan

by the romantic shadows
of the bamboo trees hide
the full moon smiling

69 Degrees

Scott Lawson

When I started tripping I don't recall
Anyone trying to break my fall
Over serve swerving
Looking up at the curb
Sixty-nine degrees
in Border Town, Texas

Shot a Tequila chasing beer
Devil's senorita whispers in my ear
"What you doing here?"
"Who left your heart so reckless?"

California girls can't beat 'em all
Oregon Angels make a man feel small
Warm your soul
Then check you off the checklist

Lone Star State knows its name
Blood stain on a kilo of
Grade A cocaine
No one to blame
Natural cause death wish

Poor the V-8 inside the brew
Thinking 'bout someone
Who ain't thinking of you
Who needs food
Who needs sleep or best friends

Sixty-nine degrees in Border Town, Texas

The Poet
Ruth Housman

the Great Archer raises
the Great Bow
straight bow
straight arrow
another peer sing
thing
straight through
the heart

Children of the Sun
Andi Garcia Linn

Children of the sun
born of soil and river
El Rio Grande
the river that looms
flows with promise
called their families north

They had no choice
At five and six
my mother and father
taken from their land of birth Pal Norte
where they did not speak the language
Sent to schools that
Refused to tolerate difference
Forced assimilation
through shame and humiliation

Violently punished by
kindergarten teachers
for speaking Spanish
the language of their birth
The language they first learned to say
"Te quiero mucho"
Chastised by adults who were
meant to welcome them
 to their new home

Though traumatized
They were unbroken
Their hearts beat loudly in Spanish
While their mouths uttered
words in private
They did not lose their language
Or the memories of their first home
Children of the sun
made of soil and river

Trauma did not hinder their growth
They found healing in creating art, poetry, teatro and familia
They still work tirelessly to spread the medicine of hope
To their community
Their roots are planted deep within this land
Sprouted children with pride in their culture
And grandchildren that cherish their Mestizo blood

The Silent Lullaby
Brandon Adam Haven

Silent dismal from eternity's sway
Cloaked in blank, wordlessly astray
Fatigued and dismayed, broken I pray
For the silent lullaby to cease away

Forbidding through the darkening night
Covered in tears, lonesome in fright
Sounds of laughter cover my cries
For they become the silent lullaby

Broken from endeavor, spent is forever
In utter horror by the demons inside
I hear the joyful festivities arise
They cover tightly my silent lullaby

Done with their conniving ways
I close my eyes then scatter my brains
Many days do pass as well as the laughs
Unheard my silent lullaby, eternally intact

I Am Just a Witness
Emma Callan

Stones in the river
Circles created
Fishes they remove
Themselves
Away for the minute
Circles within circles
Ripple from the centre
Witness to the moment
It's all part of the nature
I am just a bystander
Taking in the moment
I am just a witness
Totally devoted
I am not the author
I am the narrator
Trying to make some sense
Of the makings of our creator

An Eternity Beside Railways
Rafik Romdhani

I won't walk my heart
with my drunk dreams anymore.
Whenever it is on the loose,
it wrecks peace and starts a war.
I can't help but tie it hard
and bury it under a pile of rocks.
I won't cast my heart
like the sole dart
in the richest ocean in sharks.
But I will always write
on it the silence of a graveyard
lain like an eternity beside railways.

Romantic Poet
Steve Wheeler

Let me mend your broken heart
I'll caress it delicately
Let me help your love restart
I'm a romantic poet, see

Let me bind your emotional wounds
I will dress them carefully
I won't leave your heart marooned
I'm a romantic poet, see

You can tell me all about the pain
that hurt you emotionally
I'll get you on your feet again
I'm a romantic poet, see

Please don't ask me for solutions
to the ills of our society
All I know of is affection
I'm a romantic poet, see

A Celestial Journey
Kim Elizabeth Dawson

Do you ever stop and wonder
What happens when you die?
About your mode of transport
To your new home in the sky?
Will it be a chariot pulled by horses white
Or will it be an angel with its guiding light
It may even be an aeroplane with a celestial cabin crew
Who'll serve you meat or chicken and a glass of wine or two
If it is a liner I hope the sea's serene
I don't want to meet my maker fifty shades of green
But whichever way we get there it cannot be denied
It will be one amazing, breath-taking heavenly ride

The Poet and the Painter

John Rennie

...he wrote of things that
Meant something to him
Matters of the heart
Of the mind
The soul
She adorned her canvas
With splashed emotions
Both of them wrought
In vibrant shades of thought
A Poet and a Painter, caught
In their own time
Words and images
Created and refined
Each giving of themselves
Far too much to survive
Lost in their own time
Ahead yet so far behind
He writes with painted hands
She colours her portraits
With his words on her mind
He charges his lines
With her colourful fate
Together they will create
He will write in shades
Chasing the perfect hue
Of the unachievable
She will paint in plays
Facing imperfect blues
Together they face the studio
Of perfect light and tone
United in harmony, they know
They must face this hell alone
Their primaries and ink
Eternally combined as one
Deep and isolating colour
Holding emulsified hands
And hearts in their palette
Of creations, they turn again
From each other and commence

Their efforts to express
What they can, this art
Of images and words
Portraits of his verses
Captured in her canvas
The Poet and the Painter
Resigned to their curses.

Coal Mine Poetry
Stephane Guenette

Sticks and strangulation rope;
Wet eyelids, cracked hands;
Beating the corpse like straw.
A hard night on earth;
A treasure of countless words;
Axes and crosses.

Eight eyes and a fine finish;
The smell of sandalwood;
The bulldozer repels my arrows.
Elegance, refinement, bliss and flow;
The eye's attitude to desire and whims;
The limitless remnant of emptiness.
Forest phobias and wanderers;
The oil lamp is lit in the dark;
Shaped eyes can see it.

Crooked sentences, distorted words,
perverted behavior;
Preaching the cult of existence;
Owl wrestlers, thought ballet and fairy tale scenes.
Barking in bottles, floating in dark oceans;
Old ideas found in the search crawl;
Endless prophecies and poetic abductions;
Bloated on fictitious vibrational energy
In my handsome double-down crown.

If Only Walls Could Speak
Amanda Wilson

If only walls could speak, they'd have some tales to tell,
the memories of the past are in the panels of where you dwell.
Every word that you may utter every thought that torments your mind,
ingrains itself in the building and there it's left behind.
If generations have lived before where you now reside,
it stands to reason echoes of the past still remain inside.
Imagine then a workhouse where the 'inmates' were confined,
the nightmares seeped within those walls and there they've stayed entwined.

The undeserving paupers, the orphans and epileptics,
were locked away and hidden with 'imbeciles' and lunatics.
Every 'inmates' voice of terror every shout and scream of the sick,
never heard outside of those walls but in the blood of every brick.
In the fabric of the building some bricks are etched with names,
delusions and psychosis permeates through all the frames.
The echoes of the past reveal a haunting place to be,
a sense of foreboding from a soulless entity.

So all the walls that surround you they listen every day,
so ensure you live a happy life and be mindful of what you say.
One day in the future when your time has been and gone,
your walls they'll speak to some-one else your spirit will live on.

Into the Unknown
Brandon Adam Haven

Pillaged and war-torn, a civilization of the forlorn.
Broken and undaunted, a gathering of the haunted.
Clouds of liminal memory, despairing indefinitely.
Shattered into grinds of dust, an unfathomed mistrust.
Sheltering in utter disdain, polarized into flames.
Motionless they lay, mixed in a steep concrete grave.
Sudden death, so cold, not even one had known.
Wherein their souls have flown, deep into the unknown.

Spirit of the Lilac
Amanda Wilson

The spirituality of the lilac
the fragrance and the hue,
impassioned your soul arouses
my senses wake for you.
The misty pale lilac bloom,
the blossoms heady show,
the sensuality of my man,
the man I've grown to know.

The renewal of my love affair,
with the fragrance, oh so sweet,
the scent of you, the touch of you
make my life complete.
Your refined sense of beauty,
like the lilac standing proud,
a Celtic sense of magic,
as the sweet scent fails to shroud.
White lilacs sense of purity
and innocence it transpires,
the spirituality of the purple bloom
brings forth all my desires.

The magenta's love and passion,
your essence of my soul,
the lilac's petal tonal shades,
like you, you are the whole.
The blossom planted from a seed
so many years ago,
our tender seed was planted too
our love began to grow.

The lilac is at one with you
and you at one with me,
our love entwined,
our blossom grew
in divine spirituality.

The Angry Wind
Steve Wheeler

The wind stomped down our
quiet lane and it began to pound
It roared out in its anger as
it threw its weight around
It tore the lid right off the sky
and threw it to the ground
It punched holes in our houses
and it tore our fences down
It pelted down its deluge
and the flood rose with a din,
so we closed our doors and windows
and we took the washing in
It blew its top for ages and
we thought we'd not survive
then suddenly it ended
and we all emerged, alive
We don't know why it chose to
show its temper down our lane
but something made it angry
and it was us that took the pain
The forecast only promised
light wind and scattered showers
Now its ire has been arrested,
it's locked up behind isobars.

11:11
Jon Ware

the time of the day
magical in every way
the angels do play
spiritual some would say
believing in God's okay

Out at Night

Kevin Walton

How do a city's bricks
fuel the meander a mind takes
on a nights' long stroll?
I've trodden urban streets when only random footfalls,
moisture and mechanical things broke the silence.
Los Angeles, London, Oakland, Banjul
All, have such haunts, such denizens
On weed, hash or brown liquor, many a shape did animate,
and every rare human voice heard sounded like a plot.
Raised hairs on the necks of others
Never my concern from *any* outset,
I'd bid them a hearty "walk up, bitch"
Course plied thusly, one might've considered amendments;
night air dictated stride, not much else.
Flung far from festive,
bright moments cut from light and breeze;
these were feral, wary passings.
A caveat recalled,
"small boy carry a stone"
rings clarion, in full grown psyche.
Well known, my borne contrast;
eye tests easily revealing "outcast"
to eyes cast further, or away.
Invisibility desiring no scrutiny,
malicious notice not excluded,
but especially, from the "well intended".
Esoteric bastions, plush, near bulbous,
shielded by unreachable economies
loom, slumbering.
Dawn is a lit sliver in an
direction of the sky, ushering disdain and hard looks,
en route on a clock hand
Soon industry, endeavor, desire
with myriad lesser motivations in tow,
sponge up the masses from dwellings
Wrung now, into streets as population,
undertaking outward normalcy,
they chafe like a collar
Liquors' esters, now graduated,

arrive as urination,
and a need for rest
Another pull from a joint,
and casually blown smoke ring,
comfort this urban jackal's seeking.
Any planetary outpost will do;
It need only be free of eyes
and opinions.
At such intersection
meander becomes daydream,
that soon drops below waking,
Sleep, and daylit dreams of night ensue.

Waiting
Kenneth Wheeler

Waited through the longest days
for my loved one far across the bay.
I waited in the fiercest of storms
for the one I loved and adored.

Waited in the blazing heat of day
and bitter chilled winds of the night
I tried to swim across that bay
but strong currents drove me away.

Many weeks passed. Still I stayed
under shade for the heat to fade.
Heard no news from across the bay
and no one had good words to say.

I wasted my time, she's not coming.
There's so much else I could be doing.
I glance up and she is proudly strutting
…and her nine puppies all look just like me.

Internal Fires

Sheri Lemay

Internal fires burning
Raging out of control
A yearning to connect
With a like-minded soul
Craving the touch and attention
Of the one who's meant to be
Alone for so long
You forget how it feels
To be kept safe
To be wanted
To be enslaved by desire
As the memories return
They go beyond what they were
Realization is achieved
That you are no longer her
What has awakened is new
No longer subdued
Broken no more
What emerges while strong
Is curious
In need of a guiding hand
A strong but caring soul
Who will take control
A teacher of pleasure and pain
A provider and partner on the journey
Now that the veil has been lifted
As she realizes her darkest desires
Aren't wrong and shouldn't be subdued
But rather embraced and explored

At the Ticking of the Clock

Rhiannon Owens

The clock ticks
A pendulum swings
Like a fist,
Its shadow, foreshadowing...
Her chest is encased in a steel embrace
Her stomach clenches with each swing
of that pendulum,
Can you hear that metronome?
Can you feel the tension?
Something about to implode
With every 'Tick'
And every 'Tock'
Of the Doomsday Clock...

"... and they're off!"
A frothing, stinking pint
Thuds down onto the sticky bar
In the gloomy pub that reeks
of flatulence and desperation,
The horses gallop
Sweating, straining...
One falls — who cares?
He cheers his donkey on
Not knowing the final furlong is long gone,
And the only Ass here is reflected in
the pint pot grasped in his clammy hand...

Tick Tock,
She curls up into a ball
And cries and cries
Because she knows,
She cries and cries
For the Time that was...

Simplistically Simple
Stuart Dann

How simplistically simple.
Is the beauty of your face.
From the tiniest freckle there.
Your dimples in the perfect place.

The gorgeous smile you possess.
Makes my love for you just flow.
Softness in voice when you speak.
Telling me you love me so.

With emerald eyes that gaze upon me.
Open a door into my soul.
Your softened hand within my grasp.
A touch that makes me whole.

I feel your breath upon my neck.
As you whisper when we reminisce.
Moving very slow toward lips.
How tenderly we both kiss.

Your love feels like my temple.
To where I need to worship you.
I am not sure why you chose me.
All I know your love is true.

Glad now that you are here.
How simplistically simple it just seems.
Babes you know I love you love.
For you are the woman of my dreams.

Little King

Rhiannon Owens

I see you crouched
on a tree trunk
silent and solitary
I'm drawn by your
bright yellow eye
cold and reptilian
but oh—so compelling
like a moth to a flame
your brilliant green skin attracts
you are speckled and crested
a 'Little King'
opportunistically waiting
so patiently for the skittering thrum
of luminescent dragonfly
or perhaps a large beetle to scutter by
and maybe it is your lucky day
a small bird or rodent,
a tiny snake for prey
or perhaps you are sun-bathing
basking in your plumed magnificence
closer and closer
drawn irresistibly like a magnet
I saw you yesterday
walking on water
a King of Kings
and now you are immobile
inscrutable
and I become immobile
turned to stone
by your basilisk gaze

Out the Numbing Straits

Kwaku Adjei-Fobi

I struggle through a book
the way a bluntdumb knife
blurts through a hapless loaf of yam.
Comes out the other end
of the odyssey
stuttering nothings to nobodies.
I'm stranded,
beached at the apex of pain,
pained and estranged from Life
in a dreadful kind of way.
I am a setting son,
dulled and sullied
by the ravages of time.
Yet Pegasus.
Who are you?
I am brazen,
tested of faith,
of the African stock produced,
sodden and loamy,
productive of flora
and of fauna.
Blended to a gaudy ebony.
The clipped diction
floats and explores,
circles,
searching for expression
on solid ground,
treasured,
worth its weight in love,
out of the wreck of evasive pain,
every step...
I am emerging
from the numbing straits,
ready to live,
to love, to give,
and not
to keep!

Dawn to Dusk
Yusuf M. Khalid

doves
born lovers
friends in smiles and tears
red-hennaed feet
white-frocked, eyelinered birds
share faith, unfading as gold
fresh as the morning breeze
beautiful beams
a bride and groom
awesome alike
daylight darlings
peeking the room
Baby moon
comfortable
in mother's azure lap
shines a bright smile
enough to light Earth
It shines innocent silvery rays
against the sapphire background
of Mother Sky's nightgown
Too young to spend a sleepless night
baby moon falls asleep
and darkness befalls Earth again
it was dusky
the drowsy sun retired to bed
it was dusty
the eager wind started to set
set the mood for her night party

My Earlier Life
Faisal Justin

Rare things knew at the early age of mine
Understood the moon before its reflection
Experienced life with no hope of alive
Researched mysterious subjects of the orb
Tasted the essence of life and universe
Flavored the hearts of every human being
Identified the characters of all creatures
Mingled in a way solemn and mystic things
With the colour of sphere reflected by my eyes
Tightly pinned in my heart to be memorized

Tasted the world and knew its bitter and sweet
Suffered both physically and mentally
Life gave me more pain than I could bear
And shoved me towards the shore with the high waves
Screamed for help, whispered to the distant ears
As a sufferer of a diversity of violence
I was taught what a genuine life is
Swallowed up the world before the age of necessity
I'm a victim of inhumane treatment
For me life is a test of danger

In the Woods
Naomi Tangonan

in the woods
one becomes
in tune with the trees

its silence offers
respite to a weary soul
birds fly crickets hum

in the woods
one finds company
with one's self

Tramadol Dreams
Steve Wheeler

After-images glare
Red orange outlines flare
Weird hallucinations rare
Floating off to everywhere
Nothing what it seems
In hazy tramadol dreams
Spaced out in a yellow sky
Earth breathes out a peaceful sigh
Pain flits like a butterfly
Live forever, never die
Riding on a laser beam
In vivid tramadol dreams

Memories
Michael Lorne Miller

The day I died
do you remember?
died on my birthday
was last November
Rained all day
was a chill in the air
Alone with my thoughts
I climbed up the stairs
Thirteen stories up
is a very long way
the world I give a present
on my last birthday
I finally made it
all the way to the top
The fall didn't kill me
it was how fast I stopped
Anxiety is the devil
and depression is sin
If you suffer from both
It's hell you live in

Mistress Eclipsed

John Rennie

I've had nights
Like this
When the sun's
Been coming up
I've had times
When the moon kissed
Me on my lips
As she cursed
The dawn and
Said goodbye
Knowing she missed
The point of my
Staying up all night.
T'was only for the dawn
Oh what a beautiful sight.
There was no eclipse
Of a lunar kiss
Just my desire
To see the sun
Rise ever higher.
I have two loves
But only one lover
Mistress wanes
As another hovers
On the horizon.
Early morning's glory,
As light emblazoned
And the stars
Contrived as they
Gazed from afar
Silent and fixed
In distant impasse
Leaving this
Ménage a trois
Of planetary bliss.
Me, my god Ra
And our lunar kiss

Quarter Moon
Naomi Tangonan

winter moon
i feel your warmth
despite the cold
sunrise and the birds
sing a chorus
quarter moon
bids goodbye smiling

On Being Adored
Martin Pickard

Dark eyes intent upon me all the day,
Warm body pressed against me all the night.
With joy she leaps toward me when I wake
anointing me with kisses of delight.
My every move is shadowed in obsession
and should I chance to meet or talk with friends,
hot jealousy that boils with aggression
transforms her features till I make amends.
Returning home, she runs around in joy.
I gently stroke her silky, curling hair
and feed her treats or fetch a favourite toy.
She looks on me with love beyond compare
and promises to ever be my slave
to do my bidding if I will but stay.
I tell her firmly how she should behave
And scold each deviation from the day.
Ignoring me and everything I've said
she wags her tail and runs back to our bed

Smashing the Alabaster Box
Rob Krabbe

Too much of an anchor's pull,
as the roiling sea passes me by.
Eager to fly fancy-free and full,
calling me home: the siren's cry.
Thoughts of mounting gales,
and swimming whales, prick my spine.
My heart swells in praise for days,
at the sight of the sea and open sky.

Pharisees, and Sadducees, the
Kings and Queens, none of these
have anything on the modern-day
keepers of the coin.
Lying politicians miss the point.
Old and new temptations enjoin,
while the scavengers sit the thrones;
earth's treasures and coffers purloin.

To join their ilk is to milk
the starving, the dying, the fully
finished trying, to fluff the pillows
and couches of plutocracy, then
dishonesty be the earth's new destiny.
The hell with this, for you and me!
Alabaster dreams, and anointed kings,
the last drop of blood, they take;
and in the cake, determinism well-baked.

The ache; a dying gasp of decency,
exhaled in 1963, blame it on insanity;
Jesus boiled it down to two or three,
basic tenets to follow, not hollow out,
but love, love, love all before yourself;
the core tenet to be faced? Yes,
the answers we should have aced;
bribed the final test, the best well placed
integrity laden foibles on the top shelf.

Oh, the winds, they treacherously whip!

57

For hours I have found, to stolid, sit,
a moment on solid ground, but soon
the itch, to climb back aboard I found;
people are who they were born.
I don't rely on eyes that pitch and roll,
hiding behind the profane politics,
collecting blood right with the toll.

So turn my pockets upside down,
not a single silver coin to make a sound;
don't need a fancy home upon this ground;
promises of freedom, and prisoners unbound.
It's not the bottom line, makes me whole,
but the sun glistening on my face;
fair winds up and sweeps the sea;
I hear the siren's feverishly calling me.

My one true friend, just you see,
between the devil and the blue sea.
I consider the blessings of my life,
as I think for a moment of constancy.
I don't see a downside, honestly.
Dolphins swim and play 'long side.
We share fair wind and following seas,
and I chart an open course under the sky.

A Passing Place
Cosmic Birch

My muddled mind rose high
Above the darkened misty hold
To a place where the affected cells disperse
And the pain turns to burnished gold
A passing place
Upon the raging rivers bend
Where the delusion meets my madness
And my battered body can mend

Mr. Orange

Marten Hoyle

Starlight, and nothing rhymes with your name—
And the sky does not seem the same
Since the day you came.
I felt so much older yesterday, now I am young.
And there is a word on the tip of my tongue
I do not think has been spoken before.
But this word is my only stock and store.

A foreign call into a dream half-forgot
Is rising to the surface of what I know not:
Like a voice that burns through a song
Where only the sweetest of voices belong.
I never knew there were flowers in the snow
And the birdsong that I used to know
Has returned to my ears, as if they have flown
And I do not know if I am still alone,
I do not know if this voice is my own.

There are shadows on the walls of yesteryears,
There is still the wonder of the pain and the tears…
But there are budding and blooming branches,
And the star-shine before the dawn light dances.
It's a natural confession, a strange expression
Through the space between the light and the question
Beyond answers…what is this tale that unravels
From the memories of life and the death rattles
Of what used to be…and life of what can be again
In the pieces of the hopes that yet remain?

And when the sun comes up, I'll be sad
To know that the night that we had
Is coming to a close…but I won't be afraid
From the new stars that your eyes have made
In a sky that is new above me and you.
It's all I've ever known is to hold such a light
And I'm sorry that I could not bring you home tonight.

Poem #3
Dominic Roberts

As the light began to fade, like someone had used a dimmer
switch, the reality of blindness set in. Colours once vibrant blended
into the inky darkness and became shadows. People's faces
became shrouded in a permanent dusk, and the sun lost its glow
and withered away into an empty sky. The love I once saw
vanished into obscurity, my independence so cruelly taken away,
my life had ended, my blindness had won! Or so it thought! My
senses began to heighten, the flowers gave off the scent of a
beautiful meadow, the birds sang with the voices of angels.
Although I couldn't see the sun, her rays kissed my face like a
lovers lips, a breeze gently blew away my tears of despair. The
love I thought I'd lost was in fact stronger than ever, my heart and
my soul once again danced as one. My eyes, my vision were just
playing tricks when I could see, they were just a perception of
what I thought was reality. My independence regained through
touch and sound. I have peace in my life, my mind again a happy
place to ponder. I was back, I was alive, I was free.
Blindness, you didn't beat me!

Happy Destiny ...
H. L. Jones

Happy Destiny...
For the good seventh girl
Hell rose quietly
Heaven yet small still
Did not know how to
Stand, walk, talk, or recall
The days turned towards summer
Metallic honey
Orange with bloom
Fire red earth rust
they say we are stardust
And we *trudge* the road to happy destiny
We the little tired tv children
Microwaving, changing the channel, recording
Our own voices.

Rewind the whole tape
Fast-forwarding impatiently
Keys under the mat
Silent hours, and we *trudge*
Raised by a different media
Sleeping in our milk cartons
The high sun rocks the good
Sixth girl to the frantic west
So I can no longer
Keep an eye on the road of
Happy destiny
I always heard it in my head that way
Trudge the road to happy destiny
Corrected by the elderly child who gave
Birth to me
It has always been, as written,
"We shall be with you in the Fellowship of the Spirit,
and you will surely meet some of us
as you trudge the Road of Happy Destiny."
And so...we *trudge* the road of happy destiny
The 5th, 4th, 3rd and 2nd girl is always trying to run
optimistic but impatient
Anxiously courageous
Cautious and frozen
And still I did not know how to stand, walk, talk or recall
The days turn towards the harshest of winters
One that lasted for several years
No one went outside or hugged each other
A plague on all our houses
We trudged with our mouths covered
And fought the fear back
But we trudged
September 16th always falls on a Thursday
I have been wrong about that a time or two
And If I live to be 80 then I'm halfway down
the road
The first girl may be naïve or simple
Gullible, callow, green and guileless
8 million years in space to ponder this one thought
I must trudge the road
I will trudge the road
I will live and die on the road of happy dest…

61

Thought is the Bullet

Kristi Johns

thought is the bullet
that rests in the chamber
potential is there
along with the danger

intention's the dry run
that's hidden from view
lawless and murderous
and comforting too

what pulls the trigger
that releases the pin
that fires the bullet
that pierces the skin?

for only the heart
can twist like a rope
what once was so precious
is now so remote

feasting on passion
a love most profuse
can fashion the rope
to a love knot or noose

a jury will weigh it
consider the state
intention or lack of
determines the fate

A Symbiotic Breath in the Air

Aaron Blackie

Soul to soul, my heart cleaved
Inwardly to
The heartbeats of the sanctuary
of nature:
On a hovering ride, the eyes of my
curious soul, scanning
like a computer in for the detail
Gathering;
My poetic ears panning for the
Sensitive smells
Of the depths of the secrets that
Encircled the
Fluidity of the rhythms and vibes —
The abiding wonders
Of this Natureland...
The lonely stream
Leaps up in columns
Of dazzling spreads
In a joyful laughter,
As the ducklings
Swim in acrobatic
Display of the mastery
Of swimming...
The dewdrops
From the bathing leaves,
Softening the
Grounds for the clotting mud,
Moulding the earthworm's
Home, for the
Easy delivery and weaning
Of her young...
The hole, the nesting woodpecker
Left behind
Is becomes the water reservoir for
The bystanders and
The stay-byes
Standing by the bypass
To the pathways
Through the Highlands

And lowlands
Towards the daily demands
Of the circles of life
Before this continuum, dripping
Of nature's avatar...
Oh, what a forest of flowers in
Their variegated forms...
Flourishing under the alluring
Presence of the
Hummingbirds and the butterflies
Wings like the
Colourful designs on adoring
Carpets...
What depth of waiting
Patiently can we
Equates the horns of the
Deer, becoming
The nesting tree for the
Noisome weaver birds...
Is this some kind of neighborliness
Dancing on the extended
Branches of that which makes thick,
For that which is needful
But vulnerable in the synchronising
Scale of existence,
Together upholding the quiet progression
Of a grandiose habitation?
The interplay of interdependency
In this Kindhouse,
The Interconnectivity of varied
Leaves of species,
Basking in grand stride; the
Continuity
That goes on forever...
A symbiotic breathe is in the air —
The miracle
Of unreassembled kindreds,
kindly holding onto
The plow of co-neighborhood
And co-existence...

Frozen Delights
Naomi Tangonan

frozen delights
this winter comes
in snow-kissed ground
bare trees pay homage

I
Emma Callan

I'm a creative gift
I learned to manifest
I learned to practice over
Again on creating
Things and I live
I am a cheerful lift
I learned to smile and shift
Over and over to match
My surroundings until I
Know what I is
I am a tangible art
Realist with my heart
Dreaming in my head
As I bring the dream to life
I start
To realise what I is
Being myself is quite a gift
I can be myself
And be in alignment
With what is... I

Here

Sarah Wheatley

May angels rise
To lift low spirit
In wizened eyes
Behold God's visit

Offer feather
Mirth born touch
In wintery weather
Hold you up

Within ice tried
World, a freezing
Cross you, provide
Unweighted feeling

Your body, mind
Lift above world's cold
That aches your feet
And wears your soul

Give you rise, exist
Kin angels for time
Shying dark clouds mist
Help you see light

That past this pain
And beyond your worries
There's sun, not hail
Gone winter flurries

Show in eyes of truth
All can, will be well
Warmth can soothe
And cold shan't dwell

With pause of time
And peace of angels
All will be fine
You'll be out of danger

You'll rest in summary
Beautied breath
Of woe, you'll feel
No ember left

Held in angels grace
God's guiding hand
You'll find your way

Your feet, soft land.
...

First rest, and then you'll stand
...

I know you can
...

Take now this lift
With my heart's write, dear
Close your eyes, take drift
Let pass your fraying fear

You're okay
I'm here
...

Be at peace
Bright pastures, loving angels, stand near.

Open your eyes
The path is clear.

In the Savage Wilds

Katie Collins

Our love is sweet,
rush not the hour
for I will ride thee
to the ends of the earth, my flower,
and you may ride me
to the ends of eternity,
where we will ever be,

Thinkest thou the weeds
grow fast in thy season,
O flower of May,
the sooner they are cut,
that they may grow faster,
and each generation
more verdant the flower,
the weeds grow taller,
for we are all weeds grown
in gardens verdant,
reborn to reach
with pleasurable delight,
for the sun that has raised their light,
'willows cotton white
as snowflakes fallen
on Saturn's late April grave,
waters all the flowers of May.

I will love you slowly
in your season,
and your flowers
will never fade.

Trees Cry
Naomi Tangonan

whirring chain saws
in a nearby forest
trees cry in silence

Winter Dew
Martin Eoghan

Winter berries
dangle in misty dew,
icicle cobwebs
an inspiring view.
Over the hills,
houses of stone,
freezing fog permeates
leaving nothing alone.
Fox cubs cradle
their mother for heat,
babies wrapped in
blankets peacefully sleep.
Treading the world,
with dreams and ink,
dancing in foggy dew,
having peace to think.
writing in the cold,
yet barely able to feel,
struggling to tell if
this is a dream or real.
Easing for the mind,
to travel with the faeries,
feasting on wild nut and
winter berries.

Shepherd me, Shepherd
Rob Krabbe

Shepherd me, Shepherd.
I am a lion; I am a lamb.
Where hast thou gone,
cool, soft green fields?
Vain, blue still-waters.
The river cuts through
this paradise, gentle
rushing river, both
slow and steady,
powerful and serene.
This Eden; calls me,
this Eden, bids come
thou fables of yore!

Earth, oh Eden,
Where hast thou gone?
Comes the warring
draconian darkness;
old-school evil,
birthed from puerile
fear of the people.
Simply fought,
fields of blood;
Fields of death,
and fields of war.

Shepherd me, Shepherd.
Farmland, stifling heat,
late summer drought;
Deadly storm explodes;
This sky, rumored "under cover"
of the most darkly brooding
devil's sky in hundreds of years.
There's a twister.
The soil's purified tears
feed the woodlands,
food, toil, sustenance!
The victuals, savory.
"Home," contains all the sex,
violence, pain, and vivacious

sexy spirit of conquest!
And yes, … war.

Shepherd me, Shepherd.
I was once a young
bright eager child.
My dreams could fill
a silo with wheat.
I am now an elder of war
with strict traditions of death.
So lay me down, in
this beautiful place.
Restore me, to my soul;
gently tolling, cross shoal
and field, in black gold
caisson, beautiful, majestic,
Belgisch draft horses
glisten, as they labor;
heaving to deliver me,
to my little patch of
earth and weeds.

Call it home.
This field of battle,
becomes a trained killer,
for mere country and flag.
Call it, home.

Shepherd me, Shepherd
Who's birth was
paid for by hope?
Who's hope was
paid for by life?
Who's life was
paid for by struggle?
Who's struggle was
paid for by innocence?
Who's innocence was
paid for by war?
Who's war was
paid for by sex?
Who's sex was
paid for by birth?
Shepherd me, Shepherd.

Angel of light
Octobias Obie Mashigo

Angel of light
You are sent here on earth
To be our light,
Be light to our lives
Let your beauty shine on us,

You are always on time
With your warming rays
To warm up our bodies and soul,
Love how you light up our ways
Every morning
When you rise to erase yesterday's
regrets

You are a king,
A ruler,
Because when morning comes
Find you waiting to guide us
And rule thee blue sky,
Without you our world would be
A dark world,

O, Angel of light
Sun
Light up our lives everyday
With your cascading smiles
Be light in our lives

A Storm of Brevity
James C. Little

I am the quick warm wind that
blows in morning light.
I am the gleam in this night sky
so if I seem to dim dear friends,
please drop no tears upon my tomb;
I'm here in Heaven's dining room!

What seems like death just hides my treasures
which though shadowed be,
are what His Will supplies for me.
So they are mine, my thence unbound:
No nothing sought, know nothing found.
Our Spirits live and won't demise,
don't fret at blessings in disguise.
Puff up some wind in short swift speech,
secern your words, don't overreach.
A cloud of brevity become,
a storm compressed to smallest size
that is itself and in that glorifies.

Home Sweet Home

Shelli Lane Ireland

Darkness has become my home
My best friend, my worst enemy
My lover, my destroyer
The keeper of all secrets
Betrayer of all dreams
Full of whispers and shadows
Issues not dealt with
Shoved into corners
Supposedly left behind
Merely buried in the dust

My darkness holds and hides
The key to happiness
Slipped through a hole in the floor
Fell like a magnet to the darkened
Crippled claw, disappeared into the never
More! The beast demands, insatiable
Every thought, every feeling
All are *mine* it screeches
Voracious, never satisfied
Endless appetite for pain
Dear darkness, how I love you
When you hide me from the world, yet
Damned darkness, how I hate you

When you won't let me hide
From myself, when you release
Unhinged demons and monsters
Nowhere to hide from
All of my ugliness, it surrounds me
Seething, screaming, beyond angry
Demanding satisfaction
Let me go, darkness
For a day, a night, an hour
A mere moment in time
Relax that iron clasp, let me
Glimpse the light, take one deep breath
Show one shred of kindness, if you dare
Treacherous darkness, loves to hear me beg
Waste of breath, hopes high for nothing
Loving my pain, you trap me again in your arms
The darkness has become my home

Cicada Song
Victoria Fennell

I look into the sparkle of the eyes
Chicharas staring back at me
deep in the onyx of their bitty spheres
Popping on either side
of their gregarious green bodies
I see their calm
serenity, wisdom
They are a little girl's confidant
Land and listen intently on her hand
Exchanging glaring depth
of concern for the suffering
Sit still in the palm of her
flesh, absorbing painful memories
of Momma's tears
wiped away by her strength
Momma taught me to fight demons
fight off pessimistic feelings
how to float, flutter and fly

74

iNPrint

Sarah Wheatley

Dishevelled
Eyes level to the page I read
I'm weathered
Yet buried, full in ecstasy

Mind unravelled
To the turning of the page,
the scratch
Emblazoned,
Pictures swirl, grace second act

Take me back to before the day
Before the soul attack
Before life, mind, body,
worlds, floated away!

Forced, cast off the beaten track
Lost.
...

Yet, now, still
Encumbered
I'm happy, here, glued to my seat
Trace the numbers
Dates on photos give legs to feet

Retreating
The turn of time forms me complete
Four edges line a pathway
Circles round, and back to me.
Home, finally.

I walk forward
And picture my life

My Garden of Hope

Alexandra Xexilia Klein

After two cold Winters
my garden did not Survive
I finally have the strength
To lay down a new foundation
For my new garden

I start by ripping out
The rotten roots of my past so
I can put life back into my garden

The first plant in my garden
Is new daffodils at
A time in my life I felt
Alone and stuck
You appeared, you inspire hope and
Growth in me with your
Cloudy white petals with the
Sunny yellow break through

The next plant in my garden
Is the cactus hard to kill but
I have. This time I hope to keep you
As long as you let me.
You have always had sharp and
Protective layer over yourself but
Once you allow others in we can
All see the beauty of your blossoming
Flowers the strength of your prickled
Thorns you use to protect those you love

The last plant in my garden
Is extra special to me the sunflower
Your bright yellow petals always
Brought me so much comfort
On those extra gloomy days
I could always depend on you
Being my personal sunshine and
Bring a smile to my face no matter what
I didn't always deserve you

But you stayed your loyal ways
You stood up for me and
You talked for me when I couldn't
I'm grateful for the time I had with you
I plant you to wish you happiness.

Words are Seeds

Emma Callan

Words are seeds
Sewn in earth
Planted firmly
Given birth
To attitudes
And self-belief
To shelter
From the negative
Words are seeds
That lead to stems
If words are beautiful
Maybe then
Will flowers grow
And show in June
All the way through
Summer bloom
Words are tricky
When dressed in thorns
Beautiful roses they
Do adorn
Sharp as knives
They'll cut you down
Be careful what you spread around
Words are pods
Where seeds will fall
I know them well
I see it all
We are all experiences
From winter through to fall

Alone

Marten Hoyle

I remember laying the wreath
On the day I forgot how to breathe.
Petals fell with the rain on your skin.
Somewhere I heard a song begin
And it was if everyone and everything
In that moment waited for you to sing.

I think I'll keep dying in ways you can't tell,
Written on my lips, a poison farewell.
I do not want to say goodbye again,
But I can't bear to miss you anymore.
That is just the way it has been:
Waiting for you on the far side of the door.
I've been lost in the morning as if in the dark
On seas where no ship dares to embark:
Seeking shores in the waste of glass
As the spectral heartbeats of yesterday's pass.

Cigarettes and strangers—none of these men
Mean a thing. I just need to feel something again.
And I'm crying as if you'll watch me fall apart
And come to rescue what's left of my heart.
I thought I'd finally laid the pain of you to rest
But each day, my resolve is put to the test.
I think I'll try to pretend I've passed you and moved on
But this is a war that—try as I may—just cannot be won.
I thank the silence for making me see your silhouette
And I thank your voice for what I cannot forget.
But I am lost in so many ways I cannot feel a reason
To move on from this sombre season.
And the love you never gave was a love that felt so beautiful.
My heart belongs to emptiness now, but you still hold my soul.
And I'm wasting my time, but as long as I am alone,
I'll wait amid tears for you to come home.

The New Jerusalem
Ruth Housman

when the ugliness of
the world disappears
into a big black hole

the dust of centuries
of hate is swept away
tornado of rage

The Scream
is sucked into the depths
of hellish bracken pools

washed down into
the sewers of time
a tall vessel rises

fresh water feeds
this: a beautiful vase
is coming up from
a deeper well, renewal

as if by magic pure
white roses appear
in scented masses

all that is left of
those aeons of time
pre seeded this

melancholy peace
a circling all encompassing
feeling it was all ways

about this
a feeling of exceptional
purity

a lullaby to a sleeping
child
the rebirth, only
lonely ecstatic Love!

Joy and Sorrow
Vee Maistry

Joy and sorrow the Siamese twins
Both go together and neither wins
Deceitful and manipulating the tandem be
Like chameleons they change randomly
Befriend one, and you offend the other
For they dwell in your daily thoughts
Dancing, screeching with tears and laughter
One is always green-eyed with the other
Makes me wonder how they live together
Constantly jibbering and scratching each other
Leaving scars that makes you ponder
How to deal with their conniving escapades
Scrambling the brains and turmoil the mind
Fleeting glimpses they render, you surrender
Like a fool you condone their moods
As they revolve and rotate your head
Playing games like truth or dare

Sad Poem
Octobias Obie Mashigo

I saw him sowing a cloudy
Gown at dawn,
His eyes were reciting a sad poem
Like sun at sunset ready to set
But eyes are still scanning sunrise

Tears on the ground were narrating
His stories to store peace
In his heart and mind

Crying,
Singing
Love can be cruel sometimes,
Can leave your heart crawling
In disappointment,

80

Your finger pointing women
In a sharp way piercing through
To their hearts with anger,
Hurting them,

Saying all women are the same,

He looked at me,
His eyesight was on the other side
Of the town touring,
Searching for his lover,
Eve
Eyes spoke in silent
Letting words wed my heart,
He made me cry

As he kept on saying,
Singing,
Wish she was here to hear me
Recite this poem of love,

You came and change my heart
Now it is a soft heart with soft spot,
You poured ounce of love in it
That cured ouches that took
Away my happiness,
You have nurse it with care,
Care less was my daily bread
That made you to leave me
In tears,

Hope years of love
And seasons of love,
Will bring us together again
Someday to gather cocktails of
Kisses on each other's lips

Love and Piety
James C. Little

My heart leaps high as on a trampoline
and bounces to the rainbow's end.
And so it is in old NC and so 'twill be
in paradise when we ascend.
I'll say it twice and so it will in paradise.
The soul is one meshed with great Good
and must consistent be,
forever past and future free;
we owe His sacrifice, for me, yes we.
Let's bubble joy for all to see;
I'll show it twice, for all to see.
Your past is forebear of you now,
as dawn is mother of the day,
and glowing dust the founder of a star, of me.
Your past, your present,
and your future be all each to each
bound tight with love and piety;
and echo in eternity.

Illuminate
Vincent Blaison

A spark of light
Illuminates the path
Step forth in faith
Ripples of fates
Spread the tide
Of lives tied within
Purposeful vibrations
To create balance
Of much static
Allowing patience
To pursue
Attractions of destiny
Spirits rise to the call

O My Love
S. D. Kilmer

So loving and free;
Once you used to be.
The years have been unjust.
Since,
You have become encrust-ed,
Captured and impenetrable.
Neither a tender touch
Nor a passionate embrace
Do you, at least, tolerate.

Where has your heart gone?
Trapped within this armour of flesh?
Is this what you think is best?
Encounters with you now feel so wrong.
Inhuman.
Distant.
Untouchable.
Crucible.
So reducible.

Once so loving and free;
Come back to me!
O ljubavi moja
O my love.

. . . gone.

A Poem Shivers
Ruth Housman

a poem shivers
dropping tiny
violet stars

everywhere

83

Comedic Rain

Michael Falls

Comedic rain starts falling
Is it laughing at me?
Wash away the lines
Of decency

Might as well laugh
Or I'm gonna cry
Go with the joke
Til it passes by

Thought it might change
I must have been high
Seems I'm all wet
So I'm hung out to dry

(Into each life
Some rain's gotta fall
The edge of the knife
Has no humor at all

Humility and shame
Start to block out the sun
Comedy in rain
Laughs at everyone)

Inspire me again
Like it's never been done
Dousing all the flames
The end has begun

The rain keeps falling
Like a dark comedy
Droplets of laughter
In their disharmony

Our One Star
Fouzia Sheikh

Look at the stars tonight
As if they look back at us,
And in that moment
It will be alright

If you miss our star
I'll catch it for you
And keep in my heart
So we can share it together.

Keep holding on
As life passes by
Pain is short-lived
As we are strong.

I will hold your hand
And look in your eyes
But it is only then
That our star will shine.

Ghost in my Garden
Neil Mason

I see it every morning
As I read a magic story book under the apple tree
The ghost, a friendly spirit with a smiling outcome
Ghost in my garden, chasing morning butterflies
Segmented sunshine spots march
across a parade ground sky
I catch a reflection of a mermaid in the wishing well
A heavenly face dropped out of a cloud
Silver lining made from icing sugar
I close my eyes for a moment
Ghost in my garden had gone
No trace it was ever there
Maybe it will return tomorrow

Childhood Games
Georgia Hutchings

Stuck in my head
Hide under the bed
Under comforting sheets
Reassuring heart beats
It's safe under there
Dusty old bear
Yellow dawn break
Til no one's awake
Imaginary fun
For the monsters to come
Mythical friends
To them your heart lends
Stare at your dolls
Pray they attend
The party of imps
More tea for the chimps
Imagery creeps
Ethereally steeped
A secret game
We all here are sane
Pretend cake on the plate
Mischief at the gate
Majestic old friends
All your fear ends
To them I'm the one
The boss of the game
Door quietly chained
Plots intricately spun
Breath
And wait for the sun.

The Phases of Water
Creola Jones

Back when I still lived in a needle
and swam there in an elixir less
than feeble,
though warm like an amniotic fluid
that slowly ruined
and drowned instead of nourish me,
I saw the scars on your beautiful body
as sores that began to grow beneath my eyelids.
That image from me hid
your beauty until it became
the epitome
of ugliness and war against the spirit.
Miserably, I did adhere to it.. .
Ridges hard and ungiving crusted up
my sight
in darkness bright
with pain.
Your history was a stain
on my consciousness,
and my heart's duress
sustained all my journeys into Nothingness
where I weighed less
than air
and nothing else mattered there
but peace.

But my judgement was obese
with delusion.
The confusion
from keloids that maim
the body and the brain
heightened the insensitivity
erected between your world and me.

Then one day the morning after
a night of manufactured rapture,
I walked a secluded beach
and waded into the ocean's edge
and felt the water bleach

the fossils in my soul that had formed
a wedge
between your world and me,
your scars in time
and mine.
And your spirit spoke to me from the water,
not about your slaughter,
but about your hope
that Time never broke,
and about your power
which towers
up from the ocean floor,
forgotten no more
but awaiting resurrection
in the correction
of my elusive direction.

That day I discovered the true meaning of baptism;
and it had nothing at all to do with religion.

Your scars
are my scars,
and the history that mars
my present-day with the illusion
of elusion
is no longer an intrusion
on my peace,
but a blood transfusion
giving me release
from my apathy and shame.
'Ibutho' became my newly given name...
Warrior!

Euphoria
is found in the perspective
of the collective....

Thoughts of You
Jun Valerio Bernardo

My thoughts of you elicit so much delight
creating rainbows and sunshine
creating trickling ripples dancing around.
creating soothing music that fills every empty space.
My thoughts of you fill up my senses
like a rose in the bosom of a barren plain
like a bird gliding with so much grace
like the wind caressing every contour of my skin.
My thoughts of you turn my sadness into joy
offer me comfort when I feel weary
offer me tight embrace when the night is cold
offer me company when no one else is around.
My thoughts of you bind us more closely
no matter how distant you are from me
no matter how painful it is not to see you
no matter how eager we are to feel each other's love.

Hollow Eyes
Jack Tomlinson

What lies beneath these hollow eyes?
In our darkest of days,
We look to the skies.
No elegant beauty,
Nor fading of heart.
In the quieting of spirits
We're drifting apart.

What can we gain,
And what can be lost?
Is there life in these depths
Or the passing across?
Will salvation answer on the uprising sun,
Or will God smile and beckon you, 'Come.'

From the tiniest of seed
To the strongest of flower,
From the crumbling stone wall

To the mightiest tower,
Please don't give in.
Don't give up the fight,
As the morning is calling,
Surviving the night.
The brightest star in heaven is having its say.
Down come God's angels to take you away.

Alas,
The toughest of decisions
That should never be made,
As they switch off the machine
And your eyes start to fade.

Tears will fall,
But memories don't die.
Now, just like the angels,
You'll look down from the sky,
But not with hollow eyes,
Nor under these false pretences,
Nor being enslaved
Inside technology's fences.

Away you'll soar
Through the moonlit bay,
In the valleys of heaven,
No torment to pay.
And there you'll climb
the candle lit mast,
In elegance and beauty.
At peace at last

Paz Y Dignidad Para La Semillas

Victoria Fennell

Semillas begin in the beginning
Semillas grow to feed our hunger

Without semillas we have no trees
Without trees we have no fruit
No peaches, plums, lemons, limes
Without the mighty pecan tree
We have no pecans,
Nueces to feed our hunger
Without semillas we have no corn
Without corn we have no life, no energia
No ethanol, renewable fuel,
no feed for cows, pigs or chickens
No corn tortillas, corn chips, corn in a cup,
Popcorn, corn nuts
We cannot eat without corn
Maize to feed our hunger

Without semillas we have no plants
Without plants we have no air to breath
No vegetables, cabbage, leafy greens to eat
Vegeria to feed our hunger
Without semillas we have no flowers, roses, plumeria,
Morning glories, pansies, calla lilies, birds of paradise
Hibiscus to make tea
Te to feed our hunger
Without semillas we have nothing to begin life
again and again

Semillas begin in the beginning
Let us not see an early end
with our semillas being manufactured, genetically modified,
destroyed, stolen, held hostage
by greed
Let us pray for the protection
of God given semillas
Let us not forget
Semillas are nuestra Vida

Freedom Ecstasy
Parthita Dutta

Perhaps they felt freedom
who marched on martyrs' blood
and sacrificed self
freed the chained people
from slavery, reinstated the right
of the country.
I don't possess albatross wings
to disburden my distress and fly high
I cannot dart in rocket speed
to set a journey beyond the sky
Can I know of freedom ecstasy?

Whenever I dared to utter
what I have known as truth
through nature and nurture;
being gallant, my heart blasts
words for justice break boundaries,
regardless of ramifications
like water-reservoir floods
My free soul liberates from all bondage
of corrupt laws, myth, and stigma
in that momentary life-battle
my tongue tastes the freedom.

Beautiful Imperfections
Kristin Myron Gray

Everything about you is perfection
The perfect mess
The right amount of chaos
All wrapped up
In a package full of imperfections.
For the most beautiful things grow
Flourish, ever-changing
Adapting from weathering
All the good and bad, surviving
And in the end still a glow.

Out of this World
Charlene Phare

Stargazing across the night sky
Planetary systems fly by
Wormholes, galaxies finding love
Bright twinkling lights, heaven above

Hearts beating, complete unison
Carried among dreams, switched button
Spectacular evening shared
Frightening feeling passed, repaired

Clung tightly to each other's arms
Pure delight, wearing lucky charms
Journey continued very slow
Frosty moon, cast her shadow

Artist brush, paint flicked on canvas
Reached newest heights, blurred Atlantis
Dangers unnoticed, stones not hurled
Absolutely, out of this world

Total Affair of the Heart
Charlene Phare

Their blue eyes met across the crowded room
Swept gracefully over wooden dance floor
Sudden sweet smell of his lady's perfume
In each other's arms, they simply adore
Gently twirling, her skirt floating about
He whispered sweet nothings into her ear
Jazz band carried on playing tunes throughout
His manner, looks and posture, was austere
She had a tiny frame, petite but strong
As night ended, their flame burned very bright
Had something special, knew that they belong
Their romance started with love at first sight

Knew they never wanted to break apart
Loving their total affair of the heart

And Here We Are
Kevin Ahern

The America that I once knew
No longer in the public view
Now caters to a favored few

Merchant multi-billionaires
Peddling their modern wares
Bypass taxes to their heirs

It wasn't like this always, please
This land had opportunities
Strength in small communities

Before there was consumer ease
And trickle-down economics
There were intelligent policies

Things came from a five and dime
A vestige of another time
Now, just one click and it comes Prime

I miss those days. I miss my friends
Hot dogs, happy hours and weekends
It seemed that it would never end

And here we are

Nature's Death
Jon Ware

forests so pristine
waters crystal clear and clean
mankind's not so kind
pollutants are very mean
nature's death not far behind

A World for Her
Genevieve Ray

'Growl says the tiger'

Squeaking the child,
Will mutter words,
For animals,
That might not last,
Her growth.

'7, 8, 9, 10'

She'll count out,
An abundance,
Of illustrated creatures,
That she cannot envision,
Without bars.

'Clouds!'

She points,
Excitedly,
To a mother.
Mistaking tunnels,
Of smoke for sky.

It is a world,
Grasping at decisions.
To whether,
The pace of life,
Is worth of sacrifice,
To leave a semblance,
Of what we have known.

What will the children's books,
of my niece's daughter look like?
What will she have no words for?
What creatures becoming unicorns?
Things that are made up stories by adults.

Why Should I Change?

Benjamin Blye

What is it that you find so strange?
Is it the way that I complete my tasks?
Or is it because I wear these masks?
Instead of questioning my soul,
Why not help to make me whole?
Are you hellbent on changing my pattern
So that my mind, you flatten?

Why is it you question my DNA?
Surely, you can see I'm built this way?
Do my words make you confused?
Is your soul the one that's bruised?
My imagery might be strange,
You might well think that I'm deranged.
But if you truly took the time,
You'd work-out why this way I chime,
Because if you took the time to listen,
You'd surely see the way that I glisten.
Because to you I may just be some 'guy'
And you begin to wonder why?
My writing is acknowledged,
Probably because you only see
the parts of me that are damaged.
But if you could truly see why I write,
You'd understand what I'm saying is right,
That the path to true self-esteem,
Is learning to write like a stream.
Because when the words just flow,
That's when my mind and soul start to glow.
So leave me to be myself,
I'm happy to sit on this shelf,
Because my token speaks for itself,
And that's when my mind makes me feel
complete in the soul of oneself.

Alice [Weeps] Through the Looking Glass
Katie Collins

O what wicked angel whispered my memories
Into the ears of songstresses
When I was dressed with the wound,
And the faceless winds held the sword to my throat,
Held me to the mast,
Turned my eyes towards my myriad lies
And my uncounted disguise,
Where I lay in my death throes for the touch of one
Who I felt was unattainable
Though I knew not if I was praying to my beloved
In longing, or longing for She,
Who now dissolves these tears of mine,
O wicked angel who left me lying on the floor,
As Judas on the cross,
Cross and averse and inverted
Diving like the Sophic head first into the water,
When you left I wept,
Withdrawing your light,
Was our agelong love too great to be bound by the Law?
It raised in me a tempest to devour my sorrow
While veiled in sorrow,
How could the laws that led me to you, O beloved,
Suffer from the threat that our union provide,
Or shew man and god as a weapon to possess,
The sword of some further agent to address,
That even the law is a code,
Some form of thought, egregore, or tulpa grown too great
To live under the shadow of its master,
I threw away the auld cracked lenses,
As dead flesh heaved upon burning pyres,
To reduce them to ashes
That a phoenix may be born therefore,

The radiance of each of my fancies were spectacles,
Vessels that cracked under the pressure and heat
Of a singular beam of light, broken shells,
They were all jewelled vessels that fell to pieces in my hands.

What a smokescreen then, that I have drawn a veil

To conceal my heart's desire
By turning my attention to broken vessels,
Everything I ever adored I raised in adoration
before tearing it asunder,
the light withdrawn left the temple alone
with the slayer of men,
to enforce the law with the might of his sword,
my spectacles only revealed the fullness of the birth of
Her,
for she is a binary star, and the depth of Her is a double
throne,
where man and god together dwell,
the looking glass is made of gold, though it wear a veil of
black,
I offer her my sorrow, and the veil over my eyes loosens to
glimpse
The open lotus of apocalypse.

Colour Me
D K Gilbey

Paint me not by numbers
But instead express my soul.
Let my colours guide your brush
Shades of my unique elicit raw un-rushed
Capture my calm in soft subtle hues
Country garden lavender or pale and still sky blues
Colour my fire in the richest of reds, russet and
amber
and gold
Tempered, tenacious, brazen and bold.
Picture my strong in the strength of your strokes,
in
the depth of the contours… intent to provoke.
Mirror my need in the lengths of those lines
Swooping then stooping then stopping just fine
Of reaching an ending or carrying on
Define my indecision.. wait you can't …
your arts' done.

Write Me a Poem
Kim Elizabeth Dawson

Write me a poem, sing me a song
Hum me a tune and I'll hum along.
Tell me you love me, lie if you must
Don't shatter my dreams or crush them to dust.
Laugh at my jokes, say I look nice
Help with my coat, look at me twice.
Linger around when I'm all alone
When we are together, don't answer your phone.
Make me feel young again, pretty once more
Make my heart flutter when you walk in the door.
Ask how I'm feeling, am I happy or sad?
Lonely, downhearted, hopeless or mad?
Let me remember the Us I once knew
When days were all sunshine and the sky was so blue
Let me remember the perfect duet
That we were back then, don't let me forget.

The Kiss
Anthony Arnold

With a deep breath he said,
What do you want from me?
She said as she looked
With intense hazel eyes
Your soul

A kiss was given
Unlike anything he had ever experienced
He didn't know if he could survive
He didn't know if he wanted to

A stirring came from deep inside
Something that she hadn't felt in a millennium
How could this human
Stir feelings that no one else could

No one existed but them
Thunder and lightning surrounded them
To those around them
The power of the kiss
Was too powerful to ignore

As they stepped away
They knew
This was something that they couldn't ignore
This kiss

Villanelle #1: The Pearls of Our Minutes
Tammy Hendrix

Make not haste of life's travels before death
Learn true conditions with which you are born
Grace be to those who measure their own breath.
~

Tithings to flowers, Earth, raging storms breadth
Bring forth kinships, family, friends forlorn
Make not haste of life's travels before death.
~

Love for the sake of, warm hearts in stone depth
Be still, let flow from you to all souls torn
Grace be to those who measure their own breath.
~

Sing, spirit, into the void of life's cleft
Fill with inherent light, holy gifts worn
Make not haste of life's travels before death.
~

Be not dismayed by humanity's theft
For it's within failing we restore form
Grace be to those who measure their own breath.
~

Be forever diligent through life's writhe
Wanderlust this realm commanding the storm
Make not haste of life's travels before death
Grace be to those who measure their own breath.
~

Unknown Author
John Rennie

...and yet another cold coffee
Made for delay, on the tray
With the uneaten sandwich
For and by the writer as he
Strived for his soul displayed
This was his deepest wish
And yet another old Galois
Was lit and burned his
Trembling fingertips
Sensory things still eclipsed
Dulled and stilled, the skill
He once thought he'd witnessed
And yet another fine Bordeaux
Captured before the vine closed
Opened for a while to let it breathe
He fumbled with the darkened cork
Twisting it round endlessly and
It spun as if his thoughts
Of the great days he dreamed
When, in his vanity, it seemed
All the world worshipped at his feet
Then it all slowly, silently slipped away
Now he's passed in the street
With no time of day
As he clumsily, bedraggledly
Staggers to the store to
Replenish stocks of Galois
Bordeaux and far more
And back to his studio
His study, though
Studious no more
Everything's scattered
In the dust, on the floor
He lights another Galois,
The fourth in a row
He pulls another dark cork
And the collection grows
He reads his works over
And over and over again

"Do they not realise
How I really tried to
Explain their pain!?"
"Why don't they understand
Or listen anymore!?"
He lit another cigarette
Out of another pack
He opened another bottle
And yearned for the past.
It burned down to his
Dirtied fingers
That loosely held the
Unwashed glass
As he fell into
Another stupor
Only to dream of
And then forget
Days of glory
Far in the past
He's just
Another
Unknown
Author.

Eclipse
Lisa Combs Otto

She thought he was her sun,
but he was only interested in eclipsing her.
She craved the warmth of the true sun.
She thrives in the golden...

Yet she's lost in the shadows.

That Last Ride....
(4 Tupac Amaru Shakur)
Alonzo Gross

Did U know it was the end?,
did u put ur fear aside?,
If u could do it all again?,

would U Take—
That Last Ride?.

U chose not 2 wear ur vest,
on that night in September,
After the Fight,
U knew they would come 4 u,
2 maim & dismember,
but ur eyeZ told a tale,
of Pain,
4 longer than u would care 2 remember.
When Death was knockin did U know?—
How Much We Loved U So,
As U told Afeni,
"ItZ Ok Momma Please Let Me Go".
& in2 that other plane,
Ur Soul did Divide--------
takin with U,
The Music & Poetry,
that would remain inside-------
But Did U sense it was the end?,
& Did U Blame ur pride-------?
did u see Death as it came-?
when U took...
That Last Ride?-------.

Jamie
A.S.Writes

The day you were born
Was the happiest day of my life
You are the joy bestowed from up above
A light shining ever so bright.

I never knew of such love
So beautiful and pure
Unconditional and everlasting
Until you.

Every day's a milestone
Your first step, your first word
Your first 'I love you'
That melts my heart.

Your smile, your laughter
Your hugs, your kisses
When we play and share stories
That always makes my day.

It breaks my heart
Whenever I see you cry
And I will always be here
To comfort and support you.

You are growing up too fast
Leaving the age of innocence
I now cherish and will miss
As you enter a new phase in your life.

I will forever watch over you
And be here for you, to see you through
Watching you morph into a beautiful butterfly
To spread your wings and fly.

Of These am I

Imelda Zapata Garcia

I, am of these
My blood carries the highest form of art
The 'Flor y Canto' 'flower and song'
Poetry born in my soul, pours through my mouth
My tongue liberates the gods held captive
Tears down the blinds which covered the truth
I give freedom to hidden promises held close
In the righteous legal splendor conquest
thought to disintegrate in ashes.
Brilliant legal system, Mayan manuscripts
burned into my heart.
My clamór hails the mandatory education
Implemented by the Aztec empire, almost
singular in the world.
I sing of the medicine we yet practice as
my daughter cleanses friends who are ailing.
The faith we carry even as we pray to
God and Saints dropped in by colonization.
As the new year enters, I celebrate the
Calendar, symbol of our eternal place in
this Universe.
I tell of great pyramids which on our land
yet stand. Calling me to climb the steep
steps while I might still have reason to.
I dream of the temples, once offered
to our future.
I raise arms in unity with the indigenous
brothers, sisters who dare fight corporation
moguls like Monsanto. Fight and won to
keep genetically modified seeds from their crops.
Cultural cleansing failed to scrub the glory
of the peoples of what you call the Americas.
From the floating islands developed by my
ancestors to the Codex, to the languages
being reborn on tender tongues, a civilization
continues.
As strong as the corn stalks which grow
Throughout the world now.
Such is the strength of my heritage.

Silently Screaming
Veronica Square

No one can hear the
intensity of my tears
I appear to have lots
of confidence when
I'm really filled with
loads of self-doubt
and fear
I don't know who I
can talk to or where
I can go
I feel lost and helpless
And all I can do is let
these tears of frustration
flow
I've been silently screaming
for a mighty long time
This emotional rollercoaster
I'm on has taken a toll on
What's left of my mind
Situations keep going
from bad to worse
The moment it seems like
happiness tries to come
my way something bad
happens...I must be
cursed
So ultimately I pour all
my pain into poetry
I feel relief with each
line or verse
But the more I release,
the more I go through....
I wonder if I'll ever know
what it feels like to not
have to deal with worry,
drama or having to hold
in all the hurt
I do all I can to make
people happy, but I always

get treated like dirt
This so called life of mine
gets more hectic by the
second
I feel like I have one foot
in the grave and one ride
closer to a hearse
I got a good heart and I
try to fight the good fight...
But lately, I begin to wonder
how much all the effort is
really worth
I'm tired...
I just wanna live my life
without feeling like I'm
constantly being thrown
under a bus, or into what
seems to be an
inextinguishable fire ~

Snow Drifts Line the Gravel Road
Paul D. Anderson

Snow drifts line the gravel road.
Sculpted beauty is what's shown.
We are never left alone!
Look inside you are God's own!
Heaven isn't that far off.
It's just too bad so many scoff.

If they looked inside themselves
They'd see Heaven not some hell!
An easy thing to do, but fear
Keeps us from the God who's near!
Courageous faith must be expressed
Or we'll evolve to nothingness!
Faith within the inner life
Is not some crutch to get through strife!
It's an active force of mind.
It shows direction that's Divine!
Faith in good gives new direction.

Faith in Love leads to perfection!
God is love, do not forget!
He has a purpose not found yet!
Finite eyes can never see
All of God's infinity.
But perhaps our eyes will change.
Then the finite may seem strange!
I thank You Father/Master/Spirit
Inside there's more than feel and hear it!
Inside myself I 'will' to do it!
And so with that I'll get right to it

Cairo Quartered
Kwaku Adjei-Fobi

Bathing in the grandiose warmth
spread out among Ramses' pyramids,
the host welcomes
and shuns in equal measure
I pan for ore, sore
and inconsolable,
target-shooting, missing
and hissing commiserations
to the trounced soul
"Stay and pay homage to Mother Earth.
Zombie worms lunge for her depths!"
The smile of the baby nudges me alive...
Hail to the sperm and egg ...
fruitless multiplication!
Khmer red....divorced from sanity!
Khmer red....married to callousness
hollering deathly ecstasy!
Writhing in the eerie stench of shrouds
floating up the Nile.
...tinkering with cadaver statistics ...
a charred piece of memory
refuses to decompose —
gravely shocked eyes
can merely cry for a repose.
zombie worms lunge
for her depths...

Lunatic Moon
Michael Lorne Miller

In the not so distant future
I hope it's very soon.
I'm going to buy a spaceship
and fly it to the moon.

Do you want to know the reason?
Would you like me to explain?
The reason for this journey is
I am completely insane.

It's not so much me
It's the voices in my head
They freaking hate me
and say they want me dead

What did I do to them
to make them all this way?
Why are they so angry?
I wish they'd go away

But they say they ain't leaving
They say I'm the one to go
So I'm buying a spaceship
and they're not going to know

The ship will be expensive
We all know gas ain't free
My credit score is terrible
can you help financially?

I'll send you a t-shirt
or a moon rock or two
How's that sound bro?
Does it sound good to you?

Whatever you do
you can't tell a soul
If the voices find out
I won't get to go

World Desolation
Melanie Graves

Sun setting.
Signals feeding frenzy.
Snakes gather as the world ends.
Darkness creates shadows that blend.
All the world's troubles hang suspended.
Sickening wails and moans are unending.

How did the world get to this point?
Who allowed the devil to arrive and anoint?
Will this spiral continue forever and a day?
Is anyone left to take a stand, have a say?
What happened to decency for each other?
What happened to helping one another?

This visual should be a wake-up call.
We must be present should someone fall.
Open your hearts, maybe say a prayer.
Open your hands, show that you care.
React with kindness instead of angst.
Don't use hate as a military tank.

Appreciate everything that you have.
So that tomorrow is not your last.
Darkness can create shadows that blend.
Turn on a light, see a friend.
So as the sun is setting,
There will be no feeding frenzy.

Low
Jon Ware

all I seem to know
lost deep within my folly
is melancholy
so pitch black and dark below
never have I felt this low

Butterfly

Andi Garcia Linn

Your eyes cried out, begging
"¡Por favor no me dejes aquí!"
Here — in the dusty halls
of this neglected nursing home
Your dilapidated prison for seven lonely years

I held your powder soft hands
delicate as butterfly wings
Fragile in mine
I pictured you in your sanctuary
Your cosy bedroom
where I'd pamper you with manicures
How I marvelled at the strength of your nails
The shape and beauty of them
I'd have spent hours
Filing, and painting them
had I seven more years

Your weakened grip held me for centuries
as they callously wheeled you away
Your pain, palpable
spilling out of your flooded eyes
You let out a muted cry

Part of me stayed there
With you
In that cold dingy room that smelled of
Excrement and loneliness

Those days when sleep was your only escape
from isolation and dejection
I know you felt my spirit sitting beside your bed
Stroking your hair while you slept

We still visit in dreams
Grandpa is there
We sit, talk, eat pan dulce, sip coffee
I speak perfect Spanish to you both
We laugh remembering good times

111

The Crash of Verses
Rafik Romdhani

I sleep on the scent of hope
and my head is drowning
in the worries of my pillow
choked by the darkness
of the gloomy night.
I sleep with my arms
loose and my hands
open like two rifles
with each finger as a bullet
towards the opposite wall.
There are things that can be fought
with sleep, things like a cloud hovering
around the neck of the blue void caught
between earth and heaven.
I sleep on a sky bestrewn with scars
but dream of a land all chuckling flowers.
This house of flesh and unseen bones
like hidden pillars is where I stock
Life's lessons in different boxes
and pile up the crap of existence.
I sleep in this breathing cage
like an invisible bard you can tell
only by the crash of verses on a page.
I inhabit this body and pay the rent
for that in the form of feelings
my poems share and ask for more
of them as if poetry were haunted
by the ancient crows of metaphor.

Your Shadow
Naomi Tangonan

your shadow
plays with me
in my mind
smiling too
you never left me

Movement
Imelda Zapata Garcia

Triggered into chronicles, early in my youth
Motivated by a sense that life was misconstrued
Driven then to document what vividly, I'd seen
Decided then to well record what my dark life had been

I never thought of pledging rhymes, no diction,
no structure, no theme
Dropping lines endlessly, without a plan or scheme
Threw the scribed into a hole, too dark to call a soul
To my shock, I learned at last my sweet girl climbed in whole

She dug out the words in hiding, swallowing the pain
Sipped on succulent sweet ones, to light her own refrain
She grew into a crafty voice, she used in magic tells
By senior year of high school, she'd published quite a spell

That would be the catalyst, to my return to pen
In spite of long term slumber, my voice came there and then
My daughter's voice contagious, spurred her sister too

Soon they both then published, began asking me to
I've never thought to share my voice in circles beyond my own
Having had a platform, I've shared my share of poems

I write now as a treatment, my therapy for life
I use my voice to do what I once cried out of strife
My years in live theater, gave place for activist rage
The struggles of my people once what drove me to stage

My clamor won't be silenced, now that my voice spreads far
Inspired to keep on writing, for the course of my days is par

Darkness
Sheri Lemay

The darkness surrounds me in its cold embrace
All the while it whispers my name
With each slow step I take towards the light
Towards my escape
Towards the warmth
Towards a new life
A life free of self-hate
A life of acceptance
A life free of self-doubt
A life of confidence
A life free of the gremlin in my head
A life of quiet
A life free of turmoil
A life of tranquillity
A life free of self-harm
One more step and I can break free of this cocoon
Break free of the confining chains
One more step...
A step that never comes
Again the darkness whispers my name
Once more I feel the pull of the chains
as they wrap around my limbs
And I am pulled back into the abyss
And once again the darkness closes in
And as it surrounds me in it's cold embrace it whispers,
"You should be afraid of me."
"No," I reply. "You should be afraid of *me*."

This Love
Martin Eoghan

This love cannot hold,
a heart so bold,
turning through seasons,
without any reasons,
from heated to cold
this love cannot hold.

Resistance
Kevin Walton

Yea though I roll through
the valley of lint, resistant,
as a bowling ball of Velcro
I shall gather not a single speck;

As I read, my muse goes comatose,
as I write she awakens, oblivious;
she knows not conventions,
recently stated postulates and scoffs at rules.

A literary blizzard,
ongoing since cognition turned
to see itself in the petri dish,
rages past weary, numb synapses.

Missives, allegedly based in sentience,
litter the waking attentions
of attendees who, with sentences,
Serve their sentences.

Plying the avalanche with
a crafted detachment
that mimics sanity, scribes take on
the influence of who scribed and sold.

The pen that pens what appears
before eyes reading earnestly
moves cautiously, avoiding 'exposure',
save full digestion in minds exposed

What 'ought be read'
and how it 'ought be written'
remains unclaimed province,
with many a 'master' holding fraudulent deed

Doggerel is relative, once considered
in transparency;
each author knows their own version,
and privately decries it in others.

That muse, with proper abandon
and chaos aforethought, does indeed issue
the 'projectile vomit' that so peeves
the learned, handcuffed scribes of yore.

Irrespective of stations past, she grinds;
satisfaction of her needs
is paramount in her semi-existence.
Sated now, she releases her flow.

Versed and free,
rhymed and random;
eschewing no modus, verily,
even unto unknown, unheard rhythms.

Prophylactic of a critic,
having been raised on 'these nuts',
she offers her sword point
from behind her shield

Now immersed beyond
traditional extraction,
she ponders her pure endeavors,
and allows flatulence
to issue her report

Membrane like force field
chaperones the bubbles she releases
from whichever depth she resides in today;
never to rewrite, resistant.

The Night Scatters its Feathers
Rafik Romdhani

When will the sun set upon that mulberry tree
like a golden pigeon and teach the crows
a lesson to leave me my share?
I have a mouth that can't stand its bitterness,
and I need at least one berry every morning.

When will that song we used to sing
in my grandmother's hut and whose words
were 'laugh children, fire is wood-beaten'
come back and fill the rest of our life with joy?

When will wind come down and trifle with
wicked wolves surrounded by mountains,
Wolves whose howling no longer mean anything?

When will my hair turn completely grey
to convince you it's just a cloud of curiosity
that has descended over my head to build
a nest with my thoughts and return to its sky?

When will the sea turn to a salty blue blanket
in which I'll wrap my country and protect it
from stabs that come in the form of gifts?

When will my pen be cursed from heaven
to become a cigarette with which I write
my poems inside me, and only an ancient goddess
born with every word I feel will read them?

When will the moon fall on my shoulders
to see the caves I dug with love
and the ghosts I made soldiers of
when I slept like mountains?
Darkness is neither a siege nor black dust
when the night scatters its feathers
flying me endlessly within myself at last.

Shattered

Sheri Lemay

Tension builds day by day
And minute by minute
Until one day...SNAP!

Bruises come and fade away
Yet the damage remains
Your words cut like tiny blades
And the scars remain
You take by force
That which cannot be returned
The questions all swirl within
until she screams

Is it me?
Was it something I did?
What did I do wrong?
Could I have stopped it?
Am I really that unlovable?
Am I really that stupid?
Do I deserve this?

Your answer to these questions is always yes
Until one day the questions stop
Then you realize your goal is reached
She lays shattered and broken before you
A shell of what she used to be

The questions stop
because she knows your answer
The woman she used to be
is dead and gone
The pieces lay at your feet

Yet still you aren't satisfied
Until they are ground to dust
under your boots
Only then is your soul at peace

Dragon's Breath

Imelda Zapata Garcia

Flames soar across the sky,
landing on fresh tinder
Fields of desolate parched growth
swept up in seconds
leading to the crisp of withered vines
Vines of promise of a finer wine
Flushed into swift inferno, building high
into the winds of change
From the heavens rain
of golden sparks drop
Sprinkling hellish heaven sent despair
Growing ever closer to inhabitants
Men of saintly courage step
into the tongues ablaze
Switching to and fro
the useless means at hand
Doing battle with a dragon's breath
upon their brow
Clash of Titans on the front to save,
what man has encroached
upon this arid land

A Crypt For Her

Brandon Adam Haven

The changing aura of winter beheld
Shuddering for warmth, as crystals of white befell
Before my tired feet, livid from chaste
Winds blowing heavily, I make with haste readily
Ire burning, brightly fuming from my anguished shell
As I abandoned her and covered tightly the secluded well
Hurriedly I gasp into the deep cold mend
For she's clawing and screaming, shivering her end
Remorselessly attune, darkened wrath thick and brume
I quickly consummate my endeavors
For now past her haunting screams and the most horrible dreams
My love flourishes forever.

119

Time Marches On
Martin Pickard

The tread of marching time,
relentless, loud and strong,
is heralded by happy wren
and joyful thrush's song.
Protesting the advance
of nature's journey on
in solidarity we march
and sing of seasons gone.
Brave lions, lead the march
through ice and rain and storm
to show the Easter lamb the way
toward a summer warm.
Shall we unfurl our flags
when March blows hard again
to stand defiant in the road
resisting April's rain?
No! Drummers beat your drums.
We'll wave our banners high
and, linking arms in strength, march on
to find a bluer sky

For Maria
Andi Garcia Linn

La luna llena
Filled with hope
and the fierce love
You leave behind
Love for your familia
Your comunidad
Love for this earth
with all its complexities

La Luna llena
carries you forth
bathing us in memories

Of panza bursting laughter
warm hearted abrazos
Gritos de celebración
Sweaty nights on the dance floor
Solemn talks deep into the dawn

Your poems of perseverance
Against the pain of your ailing body heal us

We can hear the calm song in your voice
When we close our eyes
cantando palabras de verdad

Of prayer

We are soothed by the medicine in your words
 nourished by the wisdom in your heart

 we bask in the glow of your eternal light

La Luna still shines
in your absence
She offers the twilight of tears as
we release you into the cosmos
Where you continue
 to dance with the stars
Una cumbia eterna

New Day
Jon Ware

twilight in the sky
as the dawn rises nearby
turning black to blue
within an indigo hue
the songbird begins his cry

Hope
Melanie Graves

What do we have without hope?
How do we find strength to cope?
Are there magic words to say?
Are there silent tomes to pray?
Must we live life without doubt?
Must we avoid speaking out?

Must we treat others right?
Must we avoid any fight?
If our faith is strong and true.
If I believe, so should you.
Hope is not an unknown thing.
Hope can provide a song to sing.

Hope can live within the smallest belief.
Hope can make a simple life feel complete.
Hope can bring a smile amidst rain.
Hope can ease fears during the pain.
Hope is a valid concept for us all.
Hope provides the strength if we fall.

Hope exists outside ourselves.
Hope does not hide on a shelf.
Open your heart while gazing forward.
Focus your eyes while looking skyward.
See and feel the world around you.
Accept the power that pulls you through.

Do not give up when a struggle appears.
Do not give in to any useless fears.
Hope is there when you need it.
Hope fills any void that exists.
Hope is there to achieve.
Hope is there, just believe.

Hope is all around us.
Hope is the real deal…trust.

Sultry
Patrik Ryan Jones

The smell of a Chevelle,
Melting over lush swamp splendor,
Moonlighting before dusk,
Warm leather and musk,
Caressing lusciously lithe legs,
Negotiating their surrender,

One hand on the wheel,
Tasting a kiss of the steel,
The little wildflower wilts,
A passenger's squeal...

Fogs the glass,
Burned rubber stripping the grass,
Salaciously surpassed,
Giving it gas,
A horse power play,

Forever,
Are the sultry hours spent,
On a sweet summer's pass,

Desolation
Michael Lorne Miller

Desolation thrives
Suffocation breathes
Depressions crushing
the life out of me

Specifically vague
Loudly unspoken
Alone in a crowd
heart clearly broken

Orderly chaos
Clearly confused

Victory means lost
Love means abuse

Angry happiness
Seriously funny
Birthday suicide
Rich without money

Unhealing wound
Never ending pain
Suicidal thoughts
in front of a train

A Woman's Song
Pureheart Wolf

I will live life proud
Untamed and unrestrained
Our voices will be heard
Unbridled from society's norm
Do not silence our words
You may think me absurd.
I am a free spirit, like a golden bird
Racing into the fire,
Let womens' rights rise higher and higher,
We will form our own choir.
This once downtrodden woman,
Is now a fighter and is enthused with desire.
Let sisters band together
We shall shout for all to hear
We will no longer be silenced
Our voices will ring in your ears
We are women
We sing our own song
Powerful as allies
And together we band as one.

A Poem or a Pop Song....

Alonzo Gross

Whas freedom 2 the lady
With the chainz in her heart? /
Whas sane 2 the crazy
Whose life's torn apart?/
Whas youth
When the truth is,
time lets u get older?/
a grudge 2 the strong man
with Regret on his shoulderz?/.

What r dreams when,
We know we,
Will surely wake up/?
Teenage love seems,
4ever until it breaks up/.
(Well)
What good is that pastor
If he's drenched in sin?/
that boat won't get there faster
with sails & no wind/

Whas the use being rich,
When u feel so afraid? /
Of endin' up in a ditch,
from delusions u've played?/
So u run from ur light,
And u hide from ur shade/
Hopin' one day u might,
still have fight that won't fade/
Searchin' all through the night
ta find love has decayed./
So Whas the goal 2 be king,
If in death, he is mold?/

Whas the joy being God
If not one hand ta hold?/
Where's the joy being God
If not one hand ta hold?/

125

("We R all...
We R all...
just right where we belong ----/
So like,
Nothin' is right,
Jus like,
Nothin' is wrong. -----/
We R here 4 one moment,
then next moment we're gone,-----/
(jus might)
make this A Poem,
(might jus)
make this A Song------/).

Mansions of the Moon
Katie Collins

Look into my eyes
Beyond the spectrum of time
Whose irises are mansions of blue,
The spectacle of rhyme,
All about me dance the myriad shapes,
Formless feathers of colorless drapes,
Veils of lips
Towering obsidian spires,
Of the vivid gilded eclipse,
Yantras that extend beyond
The moment present,
Triangles that echo
Onward through futures rent,
Spaces not yet known by the kaleidoscopic eyes,
Veiled, dressed in technicolor disguise,
Whose form drips like paint
From a solar ingress,
To divine the contents
From the mottled mess
Forged from the data stream
Endless, infinite,
Organized chaos
Received through the prism of divine light.

Always Have, Always Will
Tammy Hendrix

Dearest Mother,
Your pain is thorny.
Infinitely, consistently, generationally
Raped of sustenance, naïveté,
You have but ash and shards left to give.
~

Look at the flesh.
Ninety-nine watching,
Twiddling thumbs, ignorant
While one masters entropy
Masked as negentropy.
Meanwhile the masses atrophy.
Planned community.
Shiv unity,
Gutting with lies and blame
To keep us apart.
~

Clandestine plots
Place condos, skyscrapers
On sacred ground,
Tax water, air, deform nourishment,
Sacrifice innocence while holding galas
To honor the fallen.
~

Dearest Mother,
Your pain is thorny.
Infinitely, consistently, generationally
Raped of sustenance, naïveté,
You have but ash and shards left to give.
~

And therein, we find you, anew.
Base to launch from,
Spread wings of fire.
Start again, unite,
Until one learns the meaning of
Egotism.
~

Always have. Always will.

My Pen
Anthony Arnold

They say the pen is mightier than the sword
In the case of blacks in AmeriKKKa
This has proven to be true
You see for every black killed in the street

The pen enabled it to be so

All men are created equal
Words written
Even though we know this not to be true
The law that was written
Said that we were not even 3/5 of a man

The pen said we could not vote
We could not own property
We could not go in the front door
We had to have separate but equal
The pen wrote these lies

You see in the hands of Jim Crow
We were chained
We had no voice
All we had was fear
All we had was death and destruction

My pen says otherwise
My pen exposes the darkness
The hatred, the times
When there was no other

No other pen for us

My pen is
The voice of the voiceless
My pen is the key of the gatekeeper
My pen

Is me

Dementia
D K Gilbey

You knew me this morning for just a short while
You called out my name and you gave me a smile
I held your thin hand and your eyes met my own
For those few precious moments I wasn't alone.

Then as I succumbed to that brief interlope
Your face showed confusion and scattered all hope.
I asked myself then as I do every day
Why this ruthless disease sees you wither away.

A short time ago when we planned our retirement
Who could have guessed that was not a requirement?
We gave our best years when our children were growing
Working so hard just to keep us all going

And now that we have time it's all come too late
Can't live out our dreams through this cruel twist of fate.
Where do you go when you sit so complacent
Looking right through me with eyes dull and vacant?

You've asked to go home and you've asked why I keep you
Locked in the 'prison' you mistakenly construe
I won't let you go to a cold strange care home
Where you'd stagnate and weaken, bemused and alone.

I promised to love you for better or worse
In sickness and health ... a vow I won't reverse.
For although you have changed beyond all comprehension
To think I'd revoke is a misapprehension.

So I'll stay by your side and I'll care for your needs
From a wife to nurse I will loyally accede
I will live for each moment we share a connection
And quietly sustain you with love and affection.

The time we have left will be short and frustrating
But when the end comes I'll be with you waiting
To you I'm a stranger you once vaguely knew
But I'll love you forever because I know you're you.

Two Black Swans
Genevieve Ray

She is danced,
In variation.
Tiptoe feet,
Replicating gentleness,
To speak,
To woo,
A hapless prince.

We play her,
Centre stage,
Raven goddess,
Or dark ingénue,
Does she actually want him?
Is she bird of a feather,
of an ambitious father?
Or another woman,
Caught in his web?

Our villainess,
In two form,
Might be victim not vixen.
In another time,
Another place.
She could be a heroine.
A duo role for sorrow.
Black tulle,
A severe warning,
About a story we do not know.

Mr Fox

Charlene Phare

Looking slender so refined
Curves in place, very defined
Prowler on constant patrol
Sometimes I'm out of control

Mysteriously creeping
Leaving my victims weeping
Don't mean any harm at all
Cannot help it if they fall

Don't kill to eat, just leave them
Flowers chewed down to their stem
Like lovers that have no heart
Devoured, taken apart

Blood sports always frowned upon
Days of hunting linger on
Don't judge and put me in a box
I'm fantastic Mr fox

The Ballad of the One-Eyed Poet

Emmelia M.

As life
finally
worth giving him
only one eye
to the inner eye of his soul,
ever since sharper,
staring at each soul.

Winter Canvas
Parthita Dutta

How far my eyes could capture
is white and white, a few stripes
of black and grey persist.
The riverbank turned white
by chilly crust like the frothy latex,
in pleat by pleat condensing
the worldly pain for a year.
The grey river streaming low
with arthritis in Aegean muse
amidst the feathery fir.
Only the feathery fir, crowned
of purity is grinning in green.
Towards the south, the sun
began the journey to pacify
devotees' yearning, as promised.
Over the horizon, his silhouette
still present in orbed red
says: "muse on my golden mirror
till I come back soon."
In that quartz radiance, which
reflects the rarest beauty of winter,
there, nature rests in an inner chamber
day crawls on the clipped radius
and few lives quietly cleanse vices
on the holy fire burning
unnoticed nearby somewhere.

Without You
Jun Valerio Bernardo

Would life still make sense?
Would there still be sunshine to creep through
my window pane?
I could not imagine
how this world spins around without you
Your love is the fulcrum of my life
lest it would have no sense of direction
Your love is the sky where I can fly
in perfect rhythm
Your love is the wind
that makes me soar beneath the clouds
I know it's not easy to trek the valleys
and the mountains of living
Nor is it easy to walk your way
when the sun refuses to shine
Without you by my side,
the sun will slowly sink
down until it fades to oblivion
Without you by my side, the rainbows
will hide its colors from the delight
of my naked eyes.
Would there be a melody in a song without you?
Would there be a rhythm
in every verse of a poem without you?
I'd rather pass on than living without you.
You are more than this mortal life I live.
Your love immortalizes what is deemed mortal
in this changing world.
Your love can turn a river of tears
into an ocean of smiles and laughter.
You are my heaven where the joy
that love brings is eternal.

The Intangible Invisibility

Creola Jones

Where were you when I needed you last summer?
When my skies turned red and the number
of loved ones I lost became far greater
than the capacity of my head
to take the maiming that went on in
my heart?

I watched light depart
unaware what I was watching,
merely noticing the stopping
of joy very suddenly one day;
and I never found out how the streets
could have holes that swallowed up
black men and women
so that when they left their home
they would never be seen again.
Standing upright.
Last summer, where were You?

I have come to overstand that seeing You
required vision honed anew
from layered darkness
peeled away like crusted scabs:
Real enlightenment rips and stabs
the consciousness into Becoming.

And Lord, You were *stunning*
at first sight! more profound
than Bible tales could ever render.
And I could know You without having to surrender
my autonomy of self;
so that accepting You was not embracing Anyone Else,
for You were me and I was You.
We both derived from The Same Grand Truth.

But You were greater by extension.
And by my human comprehension,
You were moderator, liberator,
grand collaborator, divine renovator

of the world! You were equilibrium!
Battles fought and struggles won.

Only there was no real winning,
and I didn't feel the clear beginning
of Your Bright Invisibility
when danger swallowed me
and living black was anarchy.

And sun-kissed babies still came into the world
with their spirit's sovereignty
challenged callously
as soon as they exited the womb!
Last summer, where were You?

Days were warm, nights were hotter.
Black Lives Matter chants became the fodder
for the whole world's contempt.

And You deemed not one of us
exempt from raw policing
or from trickle-down releasing
of oppression down upon our nappy head,
to perpetuate dread
and encourage those of us misled
to continue on astray,
while permitting those who slay
the spirit to be multiplied in issuing to us
demerit as our poisoned daily bread. I'm convinced —

You are not present, and that these things I've said
will vanish in thin air
where they will find *You* there,
right where you were last summer,
and Today
and Forever.

Mr. Leeman
Georgia Hutchings

The first feminist that I ever met
Was my year 7 Art teacher
Mr. Leeman
Small in stature
Shuffling around the Art block
With his fags and his stick
He wasn't as quick as a whip
But we loved him a lot
He taught us to free our minds and showed us
What's what —
Picasso
Gustav Klimt
Van Gogh
Munch
Frida Kahlo
On a chilly break time this was where we'd go,
It was warm in the art room
Sheltering from the rain and snow

He taught us to soak the images in
Study their books
I was fascinated by the chunky women
Of Beryl Cook
In seedy nightclubs giving knowing looks
With skimpy outfits getting men on a hook
He taught us to take inspiration from anywhere —
Manchester gallery
Or public affairs
The blue period
Or Mona Lisa's frown

I chose to paint African kids
with their houses burning down
See, I was already fuming at the world, even by then
And the injustice that is brought on by greedy men
I painted a nude lady with wild coloured hair
She stood vivid and bold
Stood naked in London
She didn't care

With a golden glow all
Around like an aura
Pleased with herself floating almost
Passive at the stares
Beady eyes whipping on her like lashes
Her trail burned them up
Leaving them grey and in ashes
She wasn't a god or Messiah
Just a woman filled with burning passion and fire

My wonderful muse bore of imagination
Mr. Leeman spoke :
I think you should call this piece —

'Female Emancipation'

while permitting those who slay
the spirit to be multiplied in issuing to us
demerit as our poisoned daily bread. I'm convinced—
You are not present, and that these things I've said
will vanish in thin air
where they will find *you* there,
right where you were last summer,
and Today
and Forever.

Prose 'n' Cons
Patrik Ryan Jones

Poetry is light,
From the depths of the dark,
A glow of hidden meanings,
Discovered through blind passion,
Bold enough to dare the soul to wander,
Into the mouth of freedom,
In every sense of the word,

Yet the price is a story untold,
Until the end bleeds out,
Staining the page with scars of art

Path of Least Resistance

Michael Falls

Water flows as it wants
On the path of least resistance
Trying to scale the waterfall
To the core of your existence

Take another ride on your albatross
High above those burning bridges
Ignore the mounting cost
At your conscience's insistence

Great fight for a round or two
But never go the distance
Lack the will to follow through
In the end it's all just pretence

(And only could be lost
On the path of least resistance
High on your albatross
Every day is Christmas

Where your garbage is tossed
On the path of least resistance
Blurring the lines that are crossed
Hiding your dirty business)

Will water wash it all away?
Will it leave an ugly stain?
In the end, all that stays
Are memories of words said

Still you just flow through
The path of least resistance

Volition
S. D. Kilmer

The landscape is dry, it's dusty.
Where the wind kicks up the loose dirt
of spilt words. And the air
Is thick with animosity.
One must cough or suffocate.

The atmosphere is frigid.
Where words are bitingly cold.
In places the precipitation of gossip
Soaks the ground.
If one chooses to find their way.
One would be trudging through
Large puddles of hateful and resentful moisture;
Things spewed from the mouths
Of hearts discontented.

Discontented with themselves and their lot.
Upon which they project onto others;
Often close to them
A lot of which they chose,
Because,
there are certain directions
They also had chosen
below conscious awareness.

By the map of choices made
There they find themselves;
In their misery.
So they are (not) justified to play the part
Of the Victim in this passion play of
Self-created unreality.
And yet without their victim script
Of a life of volitional discontent there would be
No passion play.
No mental illness.

And the world would be in
Universal Peace.

#Schizophrenia
Vee Maistry

A menagerie of buzzing bees
Imprisoned in the beehive of the mind
In a chaotic blur of solecism
A schizophrenic world of histrionics

Delusional and bitter in a sea of humans
Trundling with mayhem and bitterness in their wake
An aura of fatuous nonchalance rippling from the normal beings
A disease that gnaws like hungry rodents

Stripping away the vestige of sanity
Stigmatized and castaway in an island of doom
These agile beings a menace to society
An anticipated presage is their daily baggage

Chameleon Pen
Genevieve Ray

My pen is beset by emeralds,
Yet translucent when in hand.
A mystic thing that never dries,
Giving my heart a place to land.

It wants to challenge every word,
Turn its tip to every whim and want.
Less a plotted route or plan,
More an experiment on any style.

My chameleon pen loves the arts,
Wishes to venerate every age.
If there were a means to compile that joy,
It would be written on every page.

Want
Michael Falls

From a want to a need
From a cut to a bleed
And the scarce breath of life
Leaves a taste of the spite

And it burns and it taunts
Like a ghost as it haunts
Bleeding apathy
Down on me

In the dark secrecy
Where it took everything
Left a wanting
And a need

(So it wants so it takes
And it lies so it fakes
Leaves the bitter taste
Of defeat
Want to a need
I've been cut so I bleed
There's no bigger waste
Than time of need)

A desire that is left
Unfulfilled for the best
Wrap my head around
Loneliness

I don't want watered down
Version of holy ground
Insidious incomplete
What's left to believe

The Continued Transformation
Creola Jones

My gift translates the blood in my veins
into the ink that stains my brain
until it must be released
lest it become increased
as tears
accumulated over years
of pain.
I look back again and again—
wondering if I could have shifted
the awful and awesome reign
from the hands of the king
to those of the prince...
but my wondering is in vain
and I have not done so since...

Hence,
my focus
now is turning locusts
into butterflies
that aim to roam the stormy skies
with wounded wings healed by the will to rise
and devise
incredulous methods enabling *all of us* to fly!

Let nothing and no one weigh your soul
down into wastelands remote.
Despair drowns, but hope floats...
And doves cry,
but the butterfly

evolves...

Taken

Imelda Zapata Garcia

Were it yours or mine, would we remain
In mental state, sublime
Would you ride your fancy car,
while the taking chose yours, this time
Wonder what my voice might shout
In my turn of losing a part of my soul
What do you think, I should cry about
If my child were Taken in whole

Taken from shelter of love, so fine
Ripped from the hearth which was built
with that child in mind
How could my head lie at rest, I know
Even when mine thought to choose it so
He was all of fourteen at the time
That summer morning,
when peace left my side

Taken by the shine of sweet innocent eyes
Lured by the bright shiny offers of freedom
From the rules of the strict home of his life
To the streets of forgotten child's tedium

Thrown in a lion's den with no defence
Coaxed to run the asphalt jungle for a pence
Eating from the stolen bread which caught
him in an officer's cuffs

Taken to a loving home where he found
it too rough
Child of mine, he thought to know
What he learned, did not yet help him grow

Shackle free seemed a better resort
Took to the streets, to with gangsters cavort
Taken to a life of crime, which he learned
Was not meant for his kind
Street smart, never taught in St. Paul's
Wound up taken to emergency halls

Twenty one stab wounds, a broken face,
Punctured lung and a tube in place
Strangulation could not finish my son
Left for dead, he got up to run
Spared to live, like a dutiful one
Lived to serve County then God
Raised his own, never leaving their side
Vows to be home with nothing to hide

Taken indeed, but for the Grace of God
Angels returned him from the grips of a lot
What of those, the ones who get caught
Taken then turned, into visions of plots
Taken to feed to the hungry wolves
Taken to labour as Slaves on a hoof
Taken, to never again see their home
Taken as children, to elsewhere grow old

Speak to me, of the Taken!

Blue Horizons
Steve Wheeler

We are each surrounded by a raging sea
on desert islands, measuring out our days
and each of us yearns for close company,
straining eyes to penetrate the ocean haze

Inside our shells we learn the rule of distance
Bereft of intimacy, we slowly fade
Falling prey to obstinate insistence
we walk the lonely pathways we have laid

We gaze out from our rocky island shores
to wonder what exists beyond our sophistry
Desiring what the other man abhors
in blue horizons, shimmering in mystery

Thinking of You

Parthita Dutta

Yet your yellow torpid body,
like the grown country grain
in the epoch and age
spurs long-ignored senses.

Yet your trembling breath,
like the catalytic wave of hope
as the white Gardenia
on leafy growth, yields
liberal love strokes.

Yet your thermic touch transmits
the same degree of warmth,
my impetus and your impulse
alas! A leap year it was, when
you mirrored my face.

We garnered many reaped seasons
now, words are unnecessary
when our silence speaks—
debate and reasoning
turn pale and bleak.

And I win by winning you

And I fail by defeating you
there is—

    no game in between.

Stories
Anthony Arnold

There out There
Waiting
For a voice
A voice to speak them into existence

Stories

The lives of our ancestors
The pain and strength they had
Their want for freedom
And their continuation to try

Stories

The children
Whose lives were taken
In a fight that was not theirs
But then again it was

The queens
Those who took them to safety
Those who fought for freedom
And gave their lives for it

The lives
Those given
And those that were taken
By the ones supposed to protect

These and many more
Waiting
Waiting to be told
Will you tell them?

Untitled (too many)

John Rennie

Here from the earliest days
She stayed for a while
Immersed in her prayers
For a forgotten smile
And she meant so well
Standing ever so tall
As the oceans swelled
And her crest did fall
She slips and pretends
And the games never end
Or so she thinks as her
Toys return into sand
I've always thought too
Much about everything
Until my head hurts with
The despair it brings
As defences bleed
All pretences need
To be protected yet heard
As the tables of greed
Turn under their feed
And are depleted in words
You always preferred
The back door anyway
Didn't you babe?
Like that was some kind
Of tradesman's entrance
I prayed to defer to
The games that you played
Didn't I babe?
Like I was some kind
Of depraved debutant
And you, the cheerleader
Who'd have believed yer
When you said I need yer
Fingering your flowering curls
As they unfolded
And straightened
Mocked as much as remembered

As you wilted and left
Behind your wholesome world
And with no apology
Or discomfort found
You'll never be forgiven
For distorting the sound
Of every song I've
Ever sung for you
I knew all along
You could never be true.

Fascination
Vee Maistry

Is it the lapping of the waves
Or maybe the happy suds
As they embrace the shore
I am filled with drunken awe
While I binge on the beauty of the ocean

Excitement threaten to seep through my skin
And drown me in euphoric bliss
From my toddling days to present seniority
My fascination has not wavered or withered
The vast ocean and its trunks of secrets

Bewilder me with helpless curiosity
Yet a simple cruise with a luxurious ship
Or even a fishing boat on the untamed ocean
Leaves me quivering and jerking with bilious nausea
Tainting my excitement to a soggy pulp

Oh! But the tempestuous ocean still excites
And has me pondering about her mysterious ploys
Seductive and alluring like a magnet she entice
To explore and enjoy her secret delights

Accidental Love
Shelli Lane Ireland

Wanna rip my chest open & pull out my heart
Slap in something that won't fall apart
Broke that damn unwritten rule
Went & caught true feelings for you
Brick upside my head, totally stunned
Never intended to love again, sure wasn't looking
Heart closed for business, retired, out the game
Body frozen, desire long forgotten
All interest in love dead & buried
Fooled myself again

You made me no promises, told me no lies, just
Showed me that inch & my heart stole the mile
Is the connection real or instant karma gonna get me
Impossible to resist, gotta take the risk
Beyond dazed & confused, all the old emotions
Pouring over me like an avalanche
More than I can handle, forgot how to deal
Too much, too intense, too fast
Physical, emotional needs competing for my attention
Your attention, any attention, pathetic whore
Not free to make you mine
Love you the way you deserve

Would we even work, if only
This, that & the other changed
Can we accept part-time, stolen moments & secret lives
Is it enough to sustain us or would we implode
Will this accidental love be my saving grace
Or a necklace made of albatross and bitterness

Lost for a Lifetime
Darren B. Rankins

Daydreams drown the purest thoughts
that cross rainbows.

Soft melodies
that butterflies sing
in the presence of Love
overwhelm one's heart.

My love,
the scent of fresh apple pie,
so irresistible,
leaves the complexity
of how much one's true feelings
will be compelled
to lose you for a lifetime.

Sunday Aphrodite
Genevieve Ray

Woken in sea foam,
Spell binding daylight.
The first echo of mornings.
Fighting left for tomorrow,
Saving our tired for Monday.

Woken, strings of pearls.
While our son slept between us.
Sunshine lies in your scattered waves,
Botticelli would admire you in drawing.
Graceful even when snoring,
I never grow tired of this scene.

Waking my Sunday Aphrodite.
My heart swells endlessly.
For the woman you are.
For the woman you made me.
The spell I fall under
Every weekend.

Recovering You
Creola Jones

Shadows trek the expanse of your soul,
but cast no light that warms your spirit.
Music lives in InnerStories told, but you no longer hear it;
(for absence of Light blocks even sound!)
But in your journey there's a glimmer to be found...
And when you become too weary to look for it some more,
I
will
look
for
you.

And when you are too weighted down
with burdens for years you bore,
I
will
share
their
weight
too.

I will not abandon you there in the dark.
I will guard over your heart
while you mend,
be your brother and your friend.
I refuse to release you to the wind
until your wings are healed and strong again!

Never lose sight of yourself, even in the darkness.
Light exists as varnish
for the tarnished will.
Your soul is Light that woe can't kill.

We exist to help each other heal inside,
to acknowledge pain behind each other's eyes,
to chant the mantra, 'Rise!'
when anguish can be deafening,
and chaos within is threatening,
and the energies of alpha and omega

have become elusive,
no longer conducive
to ascension on your own.

I will not leave you Alone.

And 'sangomas' who have all along
infused your spirit and your ways
to bring you through horrendous days
and treachery of nights,
are still there...working in your second sight!
(Don't forget their collective might
that has been ever-present in your WarriorFight!)

Remember with me!
So that you will help us all to set you free!

Life's Holiday
Christian Pike

Dusty reels of memory
Like playing in the creek
And I can feel the summer breeze
It's laying on my cheek

The water cool, the weather warm
We rightly stayed outside
Until the coolness of a storm
And lightning made us hide

Back when we had trees to climb
And woodland trails to blaze
And with that the peace of mind
That children have always

I can almost feel it now
This summer on my skin
Oh that it were real somehow
To wander there again

Careers Advice

Steve Wheeler

I was never tough enough
to be a boxer in the ring
and there's not enough blue blood
in me to be a sovereign king
I'm probably not wise enough
to be a high court judge
and I know I couldn't be a priest
'cos I always bear a grudge
I'm much too tall to ride a horse
in the Derby or the Oaks
I have no talent to entertain
and I'm crap at telling jokes
I'll never be an actor on
a West End theatre stage
or a whizz computer coder,
even though it's all the rage
My music skills are not enough
to play the Albert Hall
and football is a no-go zone
'cos I'm always off the ball
Perhaps I was too slow to be a
sprinter on the track
and I'll never be a swimming star,
when flotation's what I lack
I'll never be a doctor,
really hate the sight of blood
and farming's a non-starter
'cos I can't stand all that mud
My fear of guns prevented
me from enlisting in the RAF
The same went for the Army
and the Navy too, by half
I could never be a teacher 'cos
my knowledge is too shallow
I couldn't be a confectioner
'cos I'd eat all the marshmallow
I'd never be a cop because
I have no criminal streak
and I couldn't be a plumber

I could never fix a leak
Lack of creativity would
prevent me painting frescos
and it's a stretch too far to think that
I could stack the shelves in Tescos
I can't drive a taxi, bus or van
'cos I get so bored with driving
and ballroom dancing's out
'cos I confuse the waltz with jiving
So I sit behind this wooden desk
sipping cups of lukewarm tea
giving careers advice, and telling
schoolkids what they ought to be

We As Droplets
Emma Callan

We as droplets of the water source
Which drips a constant drip
Which collects in cups the energy
Of which we write the script
Conversing with emotions
We never come equipped
But we find ourselves amongst the
Honesty of all of it
We as little raindrops
Connected to the cloud
We as tiny messengers
We say our thoughts out loud
We as tiny droplets
connecting to the source
Of which I find it
channelling my thoughts

O! Fire of my Fire!
Marten Hoyle

O! Fire of my Fire! Speak to me in the visions
Of unborn skies in unborn seasons.
Speak of roads where no man has trod.
Sing of prayers that never reach God:

Tell me of questions of an unanswered age,
kiss me as time turns (anew) an unknown page
In tales you never told—that you never knew
But that I shall sing to you.

Tonight is yours, if you only ask, as I implore,
As you walk, beacon of the distant shore.
And all my tears that fade into the sea
I will gather for lovers such as we.
Though many, many tears shall be.

I heard you whisper with thunder in the night
Surrounded by silence and moonlight.
I thought it was a dream of divinity,
Whose echoes would live beyond me to infinity.

Though I will die someday, and shall never feel again,
Ever you shall be my bliss and woe. My ecstasy, and pain.
Ah! I rejoice in the ache of your flame burning—
I relish the rapturous agony of such yearning.

Though I shall die, you shall eternal
Be the hunger of my torment infernal.
O! Speak to me silent as my sepulchre!
Feel my still heart and see you are there.

Tonight is yours, if you only would ask, as I implore
Of thou to love me less, that I may love thee more.

Glory and Fame

Kenneth Wheeler

Seek not for glory,
and seek not for fame,
Honour is certainly
more worth the gain.
Glory's for soldiers
to win and to wear
Their medals from battles,
and their arms to bear.
Fame is for actors
on stage and on screen,
Entertaining the crowd
for applause and esteem.
Many will seek
for their glory and fame,
And through it they hope
for new life to obtain.
Writers and authors
delight in this skill
Telling their tales
in the stories that thrill.
Many still live who
had died long ago
Resurrected on screens
via old TV shows.
Some in our history
wrought wondrous deeds
Fought battles in years past,
that happy breed.
But glory and fame
are a passing phase
While honour lives on
past the best of our days
So seek not for glory,
and seek not for fame,
Honour is certainly
more worth the gain.

ABSOLUTELY
POETRY
ANTHOLOGY
2

Author Biographies

Kwaku Adjei-Fobi is a university teacher of English language and literature at Valley View University and adjunct lecturer in academic writing at the University of Ghana. He loves nature, and all genres of music.

Kevin Ahern is a Professor Emeritus of biochemistry from Oregon State University, USA. He enjoys the spare time he has gained in retirement by writing verses, limericks, and other creative works.

Anthony Arnold was born in Tampa, Florida and now resides in California, USA. He wrote his first poem in third grade and has now authored four books and is a contributor to numerous anthologies.

Paul D. Anderson is an American poet and writer. He lives in Plainfield, Illinois.

Jun Valerio Bernardo Professor Bernardo has worked in academic philosophy for three decades. His passion for poetry has encouraged him to share his writing in several international platforms for poets and writers.

Cosmic Birch is the pseudonym of Rebecca Frawley. She is a British poet and artist who lives in Derby, England.

Aaron Blackie is a poet, novelist and blogger from Delta State, Nigeria. He believes poetry is the highest genre in writing, as it can 'touch and impact the human soul and spirit, the essence of life, nature and God.'

Benjamin Blye is a writer living in Essex, England. He has been writing poetry for a decade and has plenty of material he is looking forward to publishing.

Vincent Blaison loves writing about his Christian faith. He loves the outdoors and appreciates its true beauty. He lives in Fresno, California.

Debbie Brown writes under the pseudonym *Pureheart Wolf*, and is a regular contributor to Absolutely Poetry. She lives in North Shields, England.

Emma Callan is a British poet who sometimes writes under the nom de plume *Emmelia Verses*. She lives in South Hampstead, London.

Katie Collins is a poet, artist, and essayist living in the United States. She studied psychology and history at the University of Missouri and writes about myth, symbol and spirituality. She created the cover artwork for this anthology.

Stuart Dann lives in Plymouth, England. He says his poetry is mostly written through loss and sorrow and this helps him to release his emotions rather than bottling them up.

John Davies is a poet, songwriter and musician from Redditch, England. Known as *Grandad John*, he can often be seen performing his art online on video.

Kim Elizabeth Dawson lives on the Mediterranean island of Gozo. She writes rhyming poetry and also enjoys writing spiritual and humorous poetry. On the Absolutely Poetry Facebook group she is known as *Kit Allen*.

Parthita Dutta was born in India. She is a poet by passion and an engineer by profession. She has published her poetry in several anthologies and magazines. Her poetry expresses divine love, harmony, and peace.

Michael Falls says that writing has always come easy for him, largely intended as song lyrics, he fell into poetry by accident. He lives in British Columbia, Canada.

Victoria Fennell is a poet, artist and activist. She is an award winning author of 3 collections of poetry. She lives in Texas, USA.

Imelda Zapata Garcia published her first poetry book *Cielitos* in 2005. Her writing is available for reading on Goodreads.com. She resides in Texas, USA, and is an Admin for the Absolutely Poetry group.

Debbie K. Gilbey lives in Warwickshire, England. Writing has always been her passion but she has only recently started to take her writing seriously.

Melanie Graves has been writing poetry since 2018. Inspiration for her poetry comes from nature, life experiences, or words. In addition to writing poems, she enjoys reading, gardening, and painting. She lives in Florida, USA.

Kristin L. Myron Gray lives in Manhattan, USA and has been writing poetry since she was a teenager. She likes reading and writing poetry, and spending time with friends and family.

Alonzo Gross is an American writer/songwriter and rap artist. He is the author of three books of poetry/art: *Inspiration, Harmony and the World Within* (2012), *Soul Elixir: The WritingZ of zO* (2018), *Poems 4 U AND YourZ* (2021).

Stephane Guenette loves to evoke feeling with words. He lives in the coldest [winter] and hottest [summer] part of Canada [the prairies]. As a home care worker, he has plenty of opportunities for writing, which has become increasingly important to him.

Brandon Adam Haven is a poet and musician from Illinois, USA. He is a recovered addict who now shares his insights on learning to live through his writing. His first collection *Into the Grey* was published in 2021.

Tammy Hendrix was born in Virginia and now lives in North Carolina, USA. Her work can be found on her website *A Soul In Pieces*.

Ruth Housman is intensely interested in the stories we tell, and the intrinsic alchemy of the words themselves. As a poet and writer, she says 'words are magic clay, as clay is to clef, as in key.'

Marten Hoyle is a literary endeavor based at Eglantine West in the United States. The project is held anonymously in the hands of a being known as *Vate C. Carmen.*

Georgia Florence Hutchings is a Canadian writer. She works as a creative hairstylist and is a mother of one. Originally from Ontario, Canada, she now resides in Oldham, England.

Shelli Lane Ireland was born in northwest Pennsylvania, not far from where she lives today. She considers herself a friendly, laid-back hippie type, who lets her dark side shine through her writing, a passion recently rediscovered after nearly 40 years.

Kristi Johns is the nom de plume of author Ann Cleary. Her favourite author is Flannery O'Connor and she lives in Wisconsin, USA.

Creola Jones is the nom de plume of Khalil Somadi. She lives in Richmond, Virginia, USA, has been writing since I was a child, and says it kept her from becoming broken.

Hilary L. Jones was born and raised in Austin, Texas. She is an actress, writer and singer songwriter, and has been writing poetry since she was ten years old. She has a passion for all art, but especially the written word.

Patrik Ryan Jones is an American writer and poet. He lives in Lubbock, Texas.

Faisal Justin is from Myanmar but currently lives in Bangladesh. He is a 19 year old budding poet and writer, and humanitarian worker. Writing poetry has been his passion since 2020 but he also enjoys travelling and photography.

Yusuf M. Khalid is a teacher, writer and poet from Yobe, Nigeria. His many poetry awards include poet of the year. He has been featured in Modern African Poetry, Humayuns Editorial and Funon.

Brian Keith is from Buffalo, New York and has lived there all his life. The winters are cold but the summers are beautiful. He says that as a widower he writes because if he didn't, all the pain he endured would be for nought.

S. D. Kilmer is an internationally published poet online and in printed anthologies. A retired therapist and mediator; he resides in Syracuse, NY.

Alexandra Xexilia Klein is 19 and is a proud Queer Xicana. She is a writer, activist, and photographer. She lives in Texas, USA.

Rob Krabbe is an American poet. He lives in Kansas where he is also a publisher at *Noon At Night* publications.

Scott Lawson often writes under the pen name Ghosts Story. He lives in the lone star state of Texas, USA. His collection Ghost Story will be published by Wheelsong Books in 2022.

Sheri Lemay lives in Winnipeg, Canada, has been writing for just over a year and originally started it as a form of therapy. Through the encouragement of a good friend, she realised she could help others know that they are not alone in their struggles and that there is hope.

Sofie Linn is 11 years old and lives in Texas, USA. She is a painter and writer, and enjoys making new friends and spending time with her family.

Abril (Andi) Garcia Linn is a proud Chicana artist, published poet, teacher, and performer from San Antonio, Texas. She believes that creating art is essential to a healthy and productive life.

James C. Little describes himself as an 'old guy who writes poems for his grandchildren.' He is a family practice doctor and lives in North Carolina, USA.

Emmelia M. is Indonesian write who starting composing poems during her classical Indonesian literature studies in Junior High School in 1985-1988. Her first poem was published in a local church bulletin in her home city in 1983.

Marlo D. Mahair a.k.a. Marlo Jacobson is an American poet. Her work can be found on her *Secret Poetess* website. She lives in North Dakota, USA.

Vee Maistry is a South African poet and writer. Her other interests include learning about aromatherapy and reflexology.

Octobias Obie Mashigo lives in Wattville, near the city of Benoni in South Africa. He started writing poetry in 2006.

Neil Mason is a British poet and writer. He lives in Stevenage, England.

Martin McLoone writes his poetry under the pen name of Martin Eoghan. He lives in Derry, Ireland, and his favourite poets are W.B. Yeats, Walt Whitman and Robert Frost.

Michael Lorne Miller is an aspiring writer and poet. He says he tends to lean towards the darker side of things. He is married with three children and lives in Alabama, USA.

Lisa Otto is a clinical counsellor who teaches middle school children during the day, and yoga for adults at night. She enjoys camping, dance, music, meditation, food and nature. Poetry came to her through difficult times and she says it shaped her future, helping her to let go of pain.

Rhiannon Owens lives in Merthyr Tydfil, South Wales. She currently has four published poetry books (the 'Rhianno & Asley' series) with her writing partner, Ashley O'Keefe.

Charlene Phare is a British poet and one of the admin for the Absolutely Poetry group for which she hosts live poetry events. She is a keen photographer. Her first publication was *Pure Poetry* (2020). She lives in Devon, England.

Martin Pickard first wrote and performed poetry in the 1970's. In 2019 when he was diagnosed Parkinson's Disease he found himself writing again. He finds it both therapeutic and satisfying to write about life with a new perspective gained from living with an incurable degenerative condition. He is retired and lives in Bedfordshire with his wife and devoted cocker spaniel, Elsie.

Christian Pike's favourite quote is this: "A physicist once described life as the struggle against entropy. If that's true, then poetry must christen this achievement by being our most necessary non-necessity."

Darren B. Rankins began his writing career in sixth grade and became excited about poetry when he was asked to take part in a 1994 Poetry Slam. He has since published his work in several magazines and newspapers.

Genevieve Ray is a spoken word artist and poet who has been writing poetry for two years. Her work utilises theatre, mythology and literature. She has featured in OpenDoor Poetry Magazine and The Raconteur Review.

John Rennie is a would-be lyricist turned aspiring poet. He is the founder and Admin of the Absolutely Poetry Facebook group. He resides in Manchester, England.

Dominic Roberts is an English poet and writer. He lives in Wakefield, West Yorkshire.

Rafik Romdhani is a Tunisian writer and English teacher. His first collection of poetry titled *Dance of the Metaphors* was published by Wheelsong Books in 2021.

Fouzia Sheikh is a poetess from the Middle East. She lives in Dammam in the Kingdom of Saudi Arabia.

Veronica Square works as a freelance writer and is a newly published author under her pen name Emunah Jae. She lives in the Louisiana, USA and has been writing poetry since she was 14. Her podcast is *Elevating with Emunah Jae.*

Naomi G. Tangonan is a retired teacher who has re-sparked her love for poetry. She enjoys nature and reading. The Bible is her all-time favorite book, especially Psalm 115:1 (Look it up).

Jack Tomlinson is a renowned English poet and author of 'Behind The Mask' and 'Children Of Stardust'.

Lynne Truslove says she is new to writing poetry, and loves the escapism and the feeling of freedom it provides. Her work can be found at Aromatic Potions in the Ocean. She lives in East Sussex, England.

Brett Walker is an American poet and writer. He lives in Indiana, USA.

Kevin Walton is an American poet and author. He lives in El Segundo, California.

Jon Ware When asked for his short biography, Jon wrote this: 'I am just a man trying to find balance in an unbalanced world.'

Sarah Wheatley is a nature loving poet, author and song writer from Essex, England. Alongside writing poetry and music to promote positive mental health and writing to promote environmental conservation, she enjoys gardening, crafts, superheroes, cheesy music and most importantly, pie.

Kenneth R. V. Wheeler is a retired Royal Air Force warrant officer. His strong Christian faith is reflected in two books of poetry and short stories: *Inspirations* (2020) and *Living by Faith* (2021). He lives in Plymouth, England.

Steve Wheeler is an English writer, broadcaster and recovering academic. His roots are in performance poetry and music and he has published nine poetry collections including *Ascent* (2020), *Rite* (2021) and *My Little Eye* (2021).

Amanda Wilson is a Welsh mum of 3. She is an RAF veteran and has also worked in social services. She started putting pen to paper at the age of 15 and found it both enjoyable and therapeutic.

A. S. Writes lives in Malaysia and is a writer of fiction, nonfiction and poetry about the personal experience of travel and from living in multiple countries and experiencing a variety of communities and cultures.

If you enjoyed this book, you may also enjoy reading other titles recently published by Wheelsong Books:

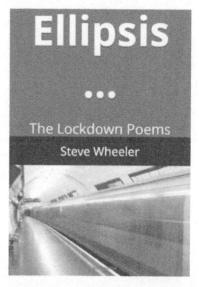

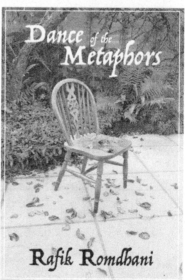

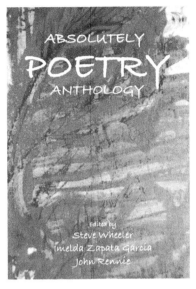

All titles are available for purchase in paperback, hard cover and Kindle editions on Amazon.com or direct from the publisher at:
wheelsong.co.uk

Made in the USA
Monee, IL
08 March 2022

92495175R10095